# ANNUITIES

## SECOND EDITION

**David Shapiro,** CFP, CLU, ChFC
**Thomas F. Streiff,** CFP, CLU, ChFC, CFS

A<sup>sc</sup>

**Dearborn**
**R&R Newkirk**
a division of Dearborn Financial Publishing, Inc.

This publication is designed to provide accurate and authoritative information in regard to the subject matter covered. It is sold with the understanding that the publisher is not engaged in rendering legal, accounting or other professional service. If legal advice or other expert assistance is required, the services of a competent professional person should be sought.

*This text is updated periodically to reflect changes in laws and regulations. To verify that you have the most recent update, you may call Dearborn•R&R Newkirk at 1-800-423-4723.*

©1992, 1997 by Dearborn Financial Publishing, Inc.

Published by Dearborn•R&R Newkirk,
a division of Dearborn Financial Publishing, Inc.®

Printed in the United States of America.

First printing, January 1997

**Library of Congress Cataloging-in-Publication Data**

Shapiro, David, 1954–
    Annuities / David Shapiro, Thomas F. Streiff. -- 2nd ed.
      p.    cm.
    ISBN 0-7931-2315-1
    1. Annuities.   I. Streiff, Thomas F., 1958– .   II. Title.
HG8790.S53   1997
368.3'7--dc20                                  96-38801
                                                CIP

# ..... Table of Contents

# ▪▪▪▪▪ About the Authors

**D**avid Shapiro, CFP, CLU, ChFC, is the principal of Shapiro Consulting Group, based in Los Gatos, California. Shapiro Consulting is a multifaceted organization specializing in investment-oriented insurance products that provides product design, marketing and sales consulting as well as technical training and continuing education to insurance companies, banks and mutual fund companies. Shapiro, a nationally known writer and speaker, has been involved with investment-oriented insurance products since 1980. He has significant experience in all aspects of the distribution of these products, most recently focusing on distribution over the Internet. Shapiro is a regular columnist for industry trade journals and has been seen and heard on television and radio talk shows. He invites readers to visit his home page on the World Wide Web at http://www.shapiroconsulting.com for current information on investment-oriented insurance products or e-mail him at annuity@ix.netcom.com.

**T**homas F. Streiff, CFP, CLU, ChFC, CFS, is president of NFC Consulting Group, a Chicago-based financial services consulting firm specializing in product design, joint venture partner searches, technical training and marketing consulting. Streiff has designed annuity, pension and life products for insurance carriers, mutual fund companies and financial institutions across the country. He has provided continuing education seminars to thousands of financial services professionals and has been a featured speaker at the AICPA conference in recent years. He is a respected spokesperson for the annuity industry and has appeared at the request of the federal government's General Accounting Office to offer his opinions regarding the taxation of annuities.

# Introduction

T he annuity is a complex product. Those of us who have been involved with this product for the past 10 to 15 years sometimes lose sight of that fact. While the annuity, as you will learn, is less driven by mortality (unlike life insurance), its investment-related aspects have required insurance company asset managers to develop complex investment strategies to meet the ever-changing needs of the marketplace.

These changes include the rapid growth of nontraditional distribution systems such as financial institutions and the advent of new and exciting product designs, both fixed and variable. These new products, including the equity-indexed fixed annuity, have crowded the field but, at the same time, they've broadened the application of the annuity product for those who seek to save for retirement and reduce the impact of taxes as they engage in that effort to save. The combination of greater availability and a heightened awareness of the annuity product has propelled annual annuity sales beyond the $100 billion mark.

In this text, we will walk through the world of annuities, exploring their origins, the development of the product and their distribution. We will differentiate between fixed and variable annuities, immediate and deferred annuities, and flexible and single-premium annuities. Finally, we will look at the marketing aspects of the annuity, examine how insurers invest for this flexible retirement product and discuss its current and past tax treatment.

Because of the vast scope of this subject matter, our discussion cannot address every particular annuity type or use. Though this text does mention how annuities can be used as funding vehicles for qualified plans, the discussion is somewhat limited. Furthermore, our focus in this text is on the individual annuity, not the group annuity. However, the individual annuity market is a large and challenging one, and you will find that this text contains a great deal of information on how to position and market annuities to this audience.

We hope you enjoy reading this text as much as we enjoyed writing it. This book represents the collective perspectives of insurance practitioners, stockbrokers, financial planners and financial institutions over a 15-year period. Your thoughts and comments are welcome, as well—in fact, we invite them. Please feel free to comment on this text by writing Dearborn Financial Publishing, Inc. We will endeavor to respond to all inquiries.

The Authors

# 1

# Introduction to Annuities

T he annuity. These two words describe a product that has seen unprecedented growth since 1980—a product that has moved to center stage, bringing with it the insurance industry. Through multiple tax law changes, an upheaval in the investment markets and severe challenges to the solvency of many financial institutions, the annuity market has continued to thrive. In just the past few years alone, we've seen a variety of new product designs and have witnessed the emergence of alternative distribution systems that have generated significant annuity volume. This text has been designed to provide the practitioner with an overview of the individual annuity market, with emphasis on how annuities are designed, how they are invested and how they differ from the more traditional products offered by life insurance companies. Armed with this information, the insurance practitioner will gain access to prospects, clients and premium dollars previously reserved for the investment specialist.

This first chapter takes the annuity back to its basic form and then brings the product into its rightful position in today's financial planning environment. We will start with the historical definition of the annuity, which would have us believe that the product is simply limited to providing an income stream guaranteed for life. Then, we will bring the product forward to a point where we can begin to understand its design and construction and how it is used today in a wide variety of financial planning applications. Throughout this chapter we will also outline the broader objectives to be achieved in this text.

■■■■■

## ■ UNDERSTANDING ANNUITIES

To understand annuities one must begin with the basics. The vast array of annuity products available for today's consumers, each designed to fulfill a unique market need or special market niche, can be confusing to practitioners and buyers alike. However, by understanding the basic design and purpose of an annuity and realizing that from these basics stem all annuity products, one can begin to plot a course through the annuity product maze. Understanding the annuity of yesterday allows for its application today.

## Annuity Principle

As most textbooks on annuities will note, the basic principle behind an annuity is the *scientific liquidation of capital*. An annuity operates to convert a sum of money into a series of payments over a certain period of time, expressed in terms of years, life expectancy or a combination of both. Though this definition reduces the annuity to the simplest of terms, it is the foundation upon which all annuity products rest (though, as you will learn, it may not be the primary reason why an annuity is purchased today). Under an annuity contract, an insurance company will convert a given sum of money into a series of periodic income payments that are actuarially calculated and guaranteed to extend for a certain number of years or for the duration of an individual's life.

Like life insurance, annuities rely on the law of large numbers and mortality and investment experience. Like life insurance, annuities protect against the loss of income. However, unlike life insurance, the focus of an annuity is not on how soon one will die but on *how long one will live*. In principle, the risk that annuity payments protect against is living too long and outlasting one's income.

## The Annuity—Yesterday and Today

Traditionally, the primary purpose of an annuity was to generate an income stream for old age or retirement. The focus was on the guaranteed payment of income and the assurance that one could not outlive his or her income. An individual would invest, say, $100,000 in an annuity in exchange for a guaranteed payment of $500 a month for life. Over the past 20 years, however, the principle behind the annuity contract has experienced a shift in focus. Insurers recognized that the market wanted products that addressed the need for the *accumulation* of retirement assets, not just their liquidation. Consequently, a new generation of annuity products was created, with emphasis on tax deferral, asset growth and preservation of principal. The annuity shifted from an income vehicle to an accumulation vehicle. The design of many annuity products was actually predicated on the assumption that the buyer would likely surrender or exchange the product for its accumulated value before it was annuitized.

Today, reacting once again to changing consumer needs and demographics, the insurance industry has taken its annuity products to yet another level. Today's annuity has become a very balanced product, emphasizing both accumulation and income. For those interested in growth or asset accumulation, as well as those needing a structured, systematic or guaranteed income stream, the annuity offers many options.

## The Purpose of Annuities

To properly position annuities and make appropriate product recommendations, the practitioner must understand that, first and foremost, these are long-term planning products suitable for those with long-term investment horizons. For most, the need annuities address is retirement. With few exceptions, they are inappropriate or inefficient for other needs or other objectives. However, the practitioner need not worry that this restricts the market—saving for retirement is one of the most pressing personal financial issues facing consumers today. The need for retirement planning and the application of annuities for this purpose is virtually unlimited.

## ■ TYPES OF ANNUITIES

An annuity is a cash contract with an insurance company. It is purchased through the payment of a single premium (in which case the annuity principal is created all at once) or through a series of premiums (in which case the annuity principal is accumulated over time). The insurer invests the premiums and credits the annuity contract with a certain rate of interest or return. The invested premiums plus the contract's growth create the annuity fund from which annuity payments are made. The funds accumulate on a tax-deferred basis, which enhances their growth.

There are many different types of annuities and many variations and options available to annuity buyers. These are explained below. Basically, the primary types of annuities can be classified by the following:

- how the annuity funds are invested (fixed or variable);

- when the annuity payments begin (immediate or deferred); and

- method of premium payment (single or periodic).

To aid in your understanding, refer to Ill. 1.1.

## Fixed Annuities

A *fixed annuity* is designed to limit the contractholder's risk, including investment-related risk, by providing a guaranteed return. This is accomplished by the insurer investing the annuity premiums in safe, secure investments, which in turn allows the insurer to credit a steady, albeit conservative, interest rate to the contract. This investment strategy enables the insurer to guarantee the annuity benefit. With fixed annuities, the values are guaranteed to the contractholder; thus, it is the insurer that

### ILL. 1.1 ■ Types of Annuities

Basis for Decision:

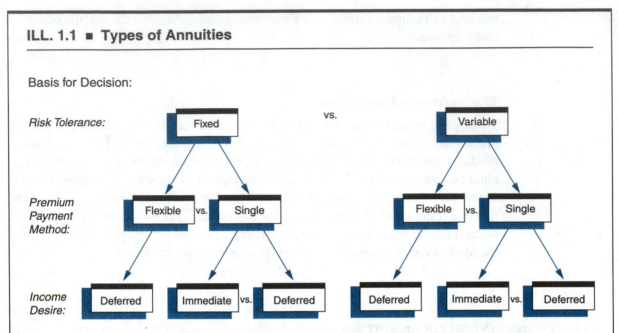

There are many types of annuities, each designed to serve different purposes and fulfill different needs. A good way to chart these different annuities is to categorize them on the basis of the prospect's financial objectives. A *fixed annuity* provides for a guaranteed, fixed return and a fixed benefit; a *variable annuity* provides for a fluctuating return and benefit, in response to its underlying investments. Both fixed and variable annuities can be funded with *periodic premiums* or with a *single lump-sum premium.* If *immediate income* is desired, either annuity can be "annuitized" and converted to produce an income stream. If income is to be *deferred,* the annuity accumulates premiums and earnings, tax deferred, until a future point in time.

assumes the investment risk. The insurer is bound to provide the contractually promised values and benefits whether or not it earns its assumed rate of return.

## Variable Annuities

With a *variable annuity,* the insurance company provides the contractholder with the option of having his or her premiums invested and managed differently. A variable annuity typically has two investment accounts: a general (guaranteed) account and a separate (variable) account. The general account provides a guaranteed return; the variable or separate account offers a variety of subaccounts that comprise stocks and bonds, which provide the potential for higher returns but no guarantees. The contractholder can determine how much of his or her premium is to be allocated to each account.

A variable annuity allows the contractholder greater control over the investment of his or her premium, but it also means that the contractholder assumes the investment risk to the extent that he or she diverts any premiums to the separate account. In essence, because they determine account allocations, variable annuity contractholders can choose how much investment risk they are willing to take. Benefits will ultimately be determined by the performance of the underlying account funds.

Because of the risk associated with variable annuity investments, they are considered "securities" and must be registered with the Securities and Exchange Commission (SEC). To sell variable annuities, practitioners must have a life insurance license and be registered with the National Association of Securities Dealers (NASD). (Variable annuities will be discussed in detail in Chapters 6 and 7.)

The choice of a fixed or variable annuity usually depends on the contractholder's risk tolerance. A fixed annuity places the investment risk on the insurer; a variable annuity means that the contractholder assumes the risk to the extent he or she invests in the contract's separate account. Each type of annuity has its advantages and drawbacks.

## Immediate Annuities

An *immediate annuity* is designed to generate an income stream to the annuitant almost immediately after it is purchased. As you might imagine, immediate annuity contracts can only be purchased with a single lump-sum premium, which creates the annuity principal. Then, within a very short time, the contract "annuitizes" and begins to generate payments to the annuitant on a regular, structured basis. Each annuitized payment consists partly of principal and partly of interest earnings on the yet-to-be-distributed account balance.

The time period between an immediate annuity's purchase and the start of the payout is usually one month, but never extends beyond thirteen months. Most annuity payments are made monthly; however, many insurers allow the annuitant to elect a quarterly, semiannual or annual payment schedule.

How long an immediate annuity will generate an income flow and the amount of each payment depends on a number of factors. Obviously, the total amount of the annuity fund is one factor; another is the distribution or settlement option that the contractholder selects. This option can be structured so that payments are made for a specified period of time, such as 5, 10 or 20 years (a *term certain* option); they can be paid for the duration of the annuitant's life (a *life-income* option); or they can be paid for the duration of two lives (a *joint and survivor* option). There are also variations of these payouts that combine a term certain option with a life income option. Given a specified amount of annuity funds, the longer the period of income payments and the more guarantees the payout option provides, the smaller the amount of each payment.

The income flow from immediate annuities can be either fixed or variable. Under a *fixed immediate annuity*, the annuitant is guaranteed an income flow without risk of market fluctuations affecting the amount of the income; the insurance company absorbs the market risk associated with the investment of the annuity funds. (There are fixed income streams that do offer some type of indexing to provide an annuitant with a distribution that, theoretically, will keep pace with inflation.) A *variable immediate annuity* transfers the investment risk to the annuitant. This means that once an income stream is created, the payments can increase or decrease based on the performance of the underlying investments.

Regardless of the payout option, the primary purpose of an immediate annuity is to create an income stream. Its function is truly that of a *distribution* or *liquidation vehicle*. Immediate annuities and annuitization options will be discussed in detail in Chapter 3.

## Deferred Annuities

In contrast to the immediate annuity, the *deferred annuity* is characterized by an *accumulation period*. In other words, there is an extended period between the time the annuity contract is purchased and when it is scheduled to annuitize. The contractholder funds a deferred annuity by making periodic premium payments on a flexible schedule or through a single, lump-sum payment. Regardless of the method of funding or purchase, the payments into the annuity accumulate over time, and each year the insurer credits the accumulating funds with a certain rate of growth or interest, which is tax deferred.

The accumulation period in a deferred annuity is usually several years. With a typical deferred annuity, the insurer guarantees the initial interest rate it will credit to the contract for a specified period, such as one year, three years or five years. Subsequent renewal rates are subject to change. Most deferred annuities have surrender charges for a specified number of years in the event the contractholder decides to cash in or surrender the contract before the insurer has recouped the cost of selling and issuing the contract.

At the point where the contractholder wishes to access the deferred annuity cash value—usually at retirement—one of three distribution options can be elected:

1. a lump-sum distribution of the entire cash value;

2. annuitization, which converts the fund to an income stream (like those described above); or

3. systematic withdrawals.

With its emphasis on accumulation and supported by a number of other unique features, the modern deferred annuity brought renewed vigor to the annuity market. Most of the innovative product designs, which generate new uses and applications, have been aimed at the deferred annuity market. As you will see, today's deferred annuities emphasize safety, asset accumulation and tax deferral. Accordingly, most annuities sold today are deferred annuities. These products will be discussed in depth in Chapters 4 and 5.

### Single-Premium Annuities

A *single-premium annuity* is purchased with a *single lump-sum premium* payable at the inception of the contract. In fact, most of the sales volume written in the annuity business today and in the past has been single premium in nature. A single-premium annuity contract does not allow the contractholder to make additional deposits into the contract; the funding of the annuity is accomplished with one payment.

### Periodic (Flexible) Premium Annuities

An annuity may also be purchased with *periodic premiums,* payable on a *flexible schedule.* For example, a flexible premium annuity might require a certain minimum initial premium—$500, for instance—but then allow the contractholder to make additional premium deposits of as little as $25 as often as he or she desires. You will find flexible premium annuities used widely to fund individual retirement accounts (IRAs) and tax-sheltered annuities (TSAs).

### Qualified vs. Nonqualified Annuities

For tax purposes, annuities are classified as *qualified* or *nonqualified.* A *nonqualified annuity,* simply, is one that is not tax qualified. Anyone may purchase a nonqualified annuity. A *qualified annuity,* on the other hand, is an annuity that is purchased as part of a tax-qualified individual or employer-sponsored retirement plan such as an IRA, TSA or other plan recognized by the Internal Revenue Service. Many of these qualified plans allow employees to fund their annuities through salary reductions. These contributions are made with pre-tax dollars, thus lowering the employees' current taxable income. These contributions then grow within the annuity on a tax-deferred basis.

The TSA market represents a significant percentage of the total annuity market. Tax-sheltered annuities, or 403(b) plans as they are often called, are reserved for very select employee groups as a way to fund retirement savings. Tax-sheltered annuities are available to public schools or educational institutions and to certain tax-exempt [501(c)(3)] organizations, such as churches, welfare agencies and research foundations. Basically, employees contribute to the plan by deferring a portion of their salaries. These deferrals are then used as premium payments for an annuity. Such contributions are excluded from the employees' gross income, thus lowering their current tax burden. And, of course, the annuity accumulates earnings on a tax-deferred basis.

The rules and regulations governing TSA plans are similar to those that control other types of qualified plans. While an in-depth study of TSAs is beyond the scope of this text, they will be mentioned occasionally, and a discussion of their application to the qualified market appears in Chapter 9.

In addition to TSAs and IRAs, annuities serve an important role in the qualified retirement market as acceptable funding vehicles for pensions, 401(k) plans and the like. Again, though a thorough discussion of qualified plans is not included in this text, an occasional reference will be made to annuities that are used for these purposes.

## ■ THE EVOLUTION OF ANNUITIES

To understand and appreciate the wide variety of financial and retirement planning applications of today's annuities, it is important to clarify a misunderstanding that has existed for a number of years. As noted earlier, the traditional definition of an annuity is one that would have us believe that it is simply an income stream guaranteed by an insurance company—that its purpose and function are limited to liquidating a principal sum of money, with the promise that the annuitant cannot outlive the income. In other words, historically, the annuity was not perceived as an accumulation vehicle, but rather as a distribution vehicle. That definition and application were reasonably accurate until the mid-1970s.

In the mid-1970s, the insurance industry introduced the surrenderable deferred annuity, with an emphasis on *accumulation* and *liquidity*. Prior to that time, annuities may have allowed for some period of accumulation, but the focus and application were on the distribution. Furthermore, early annuities had no provision for liquidity or cash benefits other than annuitization. The new accumulation-focused annuity products were based on investment spreads and asset management, concepts new to insurance practitioners. These new annuities were not as heavily influenced by the concept of mortality risk management as traditional life products, nor were they as sensitive to immediate cash flow to the annuitant, like the immediate annuity design must be. Instead, these new products focused on the concepts of tax-deferred asset accumulation and unscheduled cash flow through partial withdrawals.

Thus, unlike the annuities of yesterday whose purpose was pretty much limited to distributing retirement income, today's annuities can serve to accumulate the retirement funds, create and distribute retirement income or both. These broader applications that characterize the deferred annuity have made it by far the most popular annuity product and account for the fact that over 80 percent of annuities purchased today are deferred annuities.

## ■ ANNUITIES VS. LIFE INSURANCE

To market and sell annuities effectively, it is important to understand the difference between these products and life insurance. As noted earlier, an annuity is a cash contract with an insurance company. That means that it is a policy whose orientation to the insurer is primarily investment or asset management and, secondarily, mortality management. That single fact differentiates the annuity from the life insurance product. Unlike a life insurance policy where the primary objective is to provide death protection or estate protection for a deceased's survivors, the primary objectives of the annuity are *tax deferral, safety* and a *higher yield* than what can typically be found in a certificate of deposit (CD), money market fund or savings account. Those objectives are used by the contractholder to accumulate funds for retirement, create income for retirement or both.

Understanding the difference between asset-based products, like annuities, and mortality-based products, like life insurance, is simply understanding the different risks that insurance companies are asked to absorb by you, the professional, and by the consumer. These risks define many of the differences between life insurance policies and annuity contracts.

When an insurance company issues a life insurance policy, the company is assuming significant mortality risk. That risk is that the insured will die before the insurer has had an opportunity to earn a reasonable profit from the premiums that it has collected. To protect against losing money, the company underwrites and rates that policy, insuring as best it can that the insured will live to his or her assumed life expectancy or beyond. As such, the company is really managing mortality first and foremost. Its profits are, to a large extent, directly related to its ability to project and manage that mortality risk accurately.

Annuities, on the other hand, are primarily investment products. They have very little mortality risk. Though they guarantee a death benefit, it is usually limited to the accumulated value of the contract at the time of death (i.e., premiums paid plus interest credited). Instead, the annuity is an asset-management product by which the insurance company makes its profit from the difference between what it can earn on its investments and what it then pays out to the contractholder in the form of interest rates credited to the contract. This difference is called the "spread." Illustration 1.2 shows how the spread is determined. It should be noted that an annuity involves no underwriting, and mortality risk, while reviewed and quantified, is not nearly as important as other investment-related concerns that will be discussed more thoroughly in Chapter 10.

The primary benefits of the annuity that will be discussed in this text are:

- safety

- tax deferral

- liquidity

- probate avoidance

- yield

### ILL. 1.2 ■ *Understanding Spread Management*

**A** fixed annuity is an asset-management product. The insurer makes its profit from the difference between what it earns on its investments and what interest rates it credits to its annuity contractholders. This difference is the "spread." For example:

**9.00%** = Rate of interest insurer is able to earn on its investments

**7.25%** = Rate of interest credited by insurer to contractholders

**1.75%** = Difference or "spread" between the earned rate and the credited rate

The spread is what the insurer uses to defray costs, including agent commission, and to generate profits.

## ■ HOW ANNUITY MARKETS HAVE DEVELOPED

The nature of the annuity business has changed dramatically since the early 1970s and there is little doubt that this dynamic product line will continue to play a major role in shaping the retirement plans of millions of people into the 21st century.

When annuities first became popular in the late 1970s, they were primarily marketed as a safe alternative to a savings account or money market fund. (At that time the CD market was not nearly as large and dominating as it has since become.) Consequently, annuities were sold to older individuals who had previously kept their money in 5¼ percent or 5½ percent savings accounts with their neighborhood bank or savings and loan. As interest rates crept up and up, these savings accounts looked worse and worse, constantly being eroded by inflation. Furthermore, the interest earnings were subject to tax. With annuities, the insurance industry offered a safe, tax-deferred alternative to those products.

Over the years, the markets for annuities have expanded considerably. Obviously, the annuity is now the favored alternative to the CD. As a matter of fact, there are annuities that have been specifically designed for the CD client with a mix of short-term, medium-term and long-term interest rate guarantees to meet the various needs of the market.

Because most annuities guarantee to return the premiums that have been paid into the contract regardless of penalties, annuities are also marketed as alternatives to corporate and municipal bonds, whose values fluctuate with changing interest rates. For example, when interest rates escalate in the open market, the value of any given bond will fluctuate inversely. The higher the interest rate, the less that old bond is worth.

Thus, if a bond owner were to sell the bond, he or she could lose some of the principal that was used to purchase it. (This concept is known as "asset value fluctuation" or "market risk" and will be discussed in Chapter 8.) In contrast, a fixed annuity typically guarantees at a minimum to return the full premium or premiums deposited, even if interest rates have risen since the time the individual purchased the policy. Thus, it protects its owner against loss of principal and market risk.

The most recent surge in the growth of the annuity market came about in the mid-1990s as variable annuities and indexed fixed annuities became popular. While the expansion of the annuity market has historically come from fixed annuities and older buyers, the variable annuity has proven popular with younger individuals and has shown that it is capable of capturing assets that otherwise might have been invested in mutual funds. In addition, in a low interest rate environment, individuals who may otherwise be risk adverse have opted to take the risks associated with variable annuities to stretch for higher returns.

A new class of fixed annuities was introduced in 1992 and matured over the next few years. This class of annuities is called *indexed annuities* as they are linked to a fixed income investment such as a Treasury note or to an equity index such as the Standard & Poor's (S&P) 500. While these products add an element of concern relative to full disclosure and market conduct, the industry has readily embraced their concept as they build a bridge between the traditional fixed annuity and the variable annuity. (Indexed annuities are discussed in Chapter 5.)

## ■ ANNUITIES: AN ASSET-MANAGEMENT PRODUCT

When annuities were first introduced, there was nothing fancy about how their premiums were invested. Products were simple and their underlying investment portfolios usually consisted of high-grade corporate bonds. The average maturity of the underlying bonds was reviewed, but not held as a critical factor in evaluating the risks within the portfolio. Also not considered critical was *asset-liability matching,* which is the process of insuring there is adequate cash flow and liquidity to meet the needs of the contractholder at any given time.

As a matter of fact, most annuity carriers invested in very long-term bonds in the early 1980s, as interest rates on quality corporate bonds soared well above 15 percent. Fortunately for those carriers and the industry, the timing was right: interest rates subsided quickly, producing substantial profits to the insurance companies that invested in those long-term bonds.

Today's regulatory environment has brought about significant change to the methods used by insurers to manage their investments. Annuity carriers have set up contingencies for defaults in their portfolios. The portfolios themselves are much more diversified; they include various types of mortgages and asset-backed securities, as well as the traditional corporate bonds that still carry most of the investment weight of the portfolio.

Asset-liability matching is crucial to the performance of the annuity product today. With all of the new investment alternatives that are available for the annuity, it is vital that the insurer match cash flows of the assets with those of the liabilities. All of these concepts will be discussed thoroughly in Chapter 10.

## ■ TAX DEFERRED, BUT FOR HOW LONG?

The annuity has always enjoyed tax deferral, though over the years the government has repeatedly tried—and succeeded—in changing its tax status. This has forced product design modifications, which have had an impact on the appeal of the annuity, though continually protecting its tax-deferred status. A complete review of annuity taxation can be found in Chapter 11.

In addition to concern over maintaining its current tax-deferred status, some are questioning what a flat income tax might do to the annuity. For years, Congress has flirted with the concept of a flat tax or, more accurately, a flatter tax. Should a flat tax pass in some form, it would not spell the demise of the tax-deferred annuity. There would still be individuals who would want the safety and guarantees of the fixed annuity alone; for these investors, the added benefit of tax deferral is a secondary plus.

There is no question that future tax law changes or regulations could have a negative impact on the annuity, even though prior legislation has provided some protection through grandfathering of existing contracts. "Grandfathering" is the concession that the government makes to existing contractholders, enabling them to continue to enjoy provisions within their contracts that may not be available to future purchasers because of the tax law change.

As time goes by, the character of the annuity will certainly change. No one can predict how or when. But one thing is certain: those who wait for the possible change by procrastinating will pay a significant price. Tax law changes rarely inure to the benefit of the taxpayer.

## ■ SUMMARY

This first chapter was designed to provide a blueprint of where we will be taking you on our study of annuities. We have reviewed the basic form and principle of the annuity, including some of the misconceptions that exist among consumers and distributors alike, and previewed some of the topics that we will be discussing more thoroughly later in the text. Over the past 15 to 20 years, the annuity has changed dramatically. Investment philosophies, distribution, marketing and product design have all grown with the expansion of the market and the development of new and more suitable investment vehicles. But while the market has grown and the products have changed, the focus for the annuity has been constant. The annuity remains one of the only safe, tax-deferred methods of accumulating retirement assets. The rest of this text is dedicated to explaining how the annuity works and how it can be of benefit to the financial services professional and his or her clients.

## ■ CHAPTER 1 QUESTIONS FOR REVIEW

1. The historical definition of the annuity focused primarily on tax-deferred accumulation.

   *True* or *False*

2. The primary purpose of an immediate annuity is to provide tax-advantaged income to an annuitant.

   *True* or *False*

3. A fixed annuity is characterized by a provision allowing the contractholder to choose from a variety of mutual fund options for the investment of his or her premiums.

   *True* or *False*

4. Which phrase best describes the annuity?

   a. A life insurance policy that accumulates values on a tax-deferred basis
   b. A money market account that offers check writing privileges
   c. A contract issued by an insurance company to allow for tax-deferred growth for retirement
   d. A stock certificate issued by an insurance company

5. Which of the following is NOT a distribution option from a deferred annuity?

   a. Conversion to a life insurance policy
   b. Lump-sum payout
   c. Annuitization
   d. Periodic withdrawals

# 2

# The History of Annuity Distribution

A ny good historian will tell you that the best way to plan for the future is to examine the past. It is with an eye toward preserving the annuity that we take a look at how the annuity developed, where it stands today relative to life insurance products and how annuity distribution has grown since the first modern deferred annuity was sold in 1973. Since the growth of the annuity primarily has been attributed to the accumulation and liquidity aspects of the deferred annuity, we will focus on the deferred annuity in this chapter.

The annuity product line has experienced incredible growth over the past decade. This growth was initially fueled by the fixed annuity business; however, in 1993, the variable annuity business began to catch fire, with sales exceeding $50 billion in 1995. According to the American Council of Life Insurance, total annuity sales were $6.3 billion in 1980, $58.5 billion in 1991 and $100 billion in 1995. Today, annuity premiums account for roughly one-third of total income received by insurance companies. This unprecedented growth occurred for a number of reasons. The purpose of this chapter is to explain those reasons, track the history of the annuity business and ultimately, provide a foundation for understanding the products and purchasers that compose this dynamic, evolving market.

■ ■ ■ ■ ■

## ■ PRODUCT HISTORY

Until the early 1970s, an annuity was almost always defined and used as an income vehicle. However, all of this changed when the first surrenderable deferred annuity was developed in 1973. The earliest form of the surrenderable deferred annuity was fairly simple. The product offered a competitive first-year interest rate, with a minimum guaranteed rate that was consistent or higher than the after-tax rate of return on a traditional savings account. There was no renewal interest rate protection for the consumer, and there was typically a 7 percent to 10 percent permanent surrender charge in the contract, which could only be avoided through annuitization. The product contained no life insurance and, unlike annuity products prior to its introduction, did not require annuitization. Settlement options available at the time allowed for the conversion of the deferred annuity into an immediate annuity, where the annuitant could choose between distributions over a fixed period of time (term certain annuitization) or distributions over a lifetime (life annuitization).

Because of the investment nature of this new deferred annuity product and the perception that commissions on its sales were low, life insurance agents were generally not interested in selling the product. Remember that in the 1970s, life agents were trained to collect hundreds and thousands of dollars, not tens of thousands and hundreds of thousands of dollars. But the insurance industry saw the value of asset-management products and wanted to move into these vehicles as a balance to the other, more traditional lines of business that insurance companies had built over the decades.

## Distribution Through Stockbrokers

In addition to the new market created by these annuity products, many insurers were searching for new forms of distribution. One distribution channel that offered great initial appeal included the stockbrokers of the New York Stock Exchange (NYSE) member firms. Ultimately, the industry turned to these stockbrokers, or "wire houses" as they're sometimes called, as the primary source of distribution for this new deferred annuity product.

While the managements of the NYSE member firms were extremely interested in selling these annuities and developing this ancillary profit center, the stockbrokers themselves were somewhat resistant to beginning the marketing effort. Stockbrokers, for the most part, were not involved with insurance sales, primarily because of a lack of training and understanding. However, over a period of several years, the insurance industry and the stockbrokerage industry finally learned how to communicate with each other. The result was the blossoming—some would say explosion— of the annuity business.

Once the large national wire houses began to enjoy success in marketing annuities, the smaller regional brokerage firms came into the fold. This increased awareness of the annuity in the minds of the consumer and the insurance practitioner as well.

Because of the nature of their relationship, the stockbroker was certainly in a better position to convince the client to purchase an annuity. Stockbrokers had built their relationships based on the management of the client's assets, focusing on the client's balance sheet and all of his or her assets. That approach is different from the traditional role played by the insurance agent, whose primary focus had been estate and asset protection funded through the client's current income. (This concept of selling annuities by analyzing the balance sheet will be discussed in Chapter 9.)

There is nothing like competition to motivate and expand a market. The early and mid-1980s saw a tremendous increase in annuity sales, in part because of this diversification of distribution, but primarily because of unprecedentedly high interest rates. The economic environment of the early 1980s produced annuity interest rates in excess of 15 percent and companies issuing annuities could not keep up with consumer demand.

Unfortunately, there were some tough lessons learned during those times. Annuities began to be sold purely on the basis of the interest rate and not on the product's many other beneficial features. Then, of course, came a stabilizing of the economy, a fall in interest rates, the failure of Baldwin-United and Charter Security Life and other scares.

## Difficult Time for Carriers

The road of growth for annuity business has been a fairly smooth one. That said, there have been a few potholes that the industry has had to fill along the way. Those potholes came in two different periods: the early 1980s, punctuated by the failure of Baldwin-United and Charter Security, and the early 1990s, with the failure of First Executive Life and First Capital Holding's life companies, including Fidelity Bankers and First Capital Life.

### The Fall of Baldwin-United

Baldwin-United wrote most of its annuity business through two insurance subsidiaries: National Investors Life and University Life. Their preferred form of distribution was the national and regional wire houses. In addition to the wire houses, the Baldwin subsidiaries were also very active in the TSA market. Distribution in the TSA market was handled through the large, specialized distributors that have evolved in that market over the years.

Annuity sales from 1979 to 1982 were brisk, to say the least. In addition to inordinately high interest rates in 1981 and 1982, the annuity also enjoyed an important tax advantage: at that time any annuity sold was granted "first in, first out" (FIFO) tax treatment. That meant that in addition to enjoying tax deferral on accumulation, individuals who took withdrawals from their annuity contracts were deemed to receive first the nontaxable return of premium principal and second, the taxable interest. (This tax advantage was subsequently lost in the Tax Equity and Fiscal Responsibility Act of 1982.)

The early 1980s saw the deferred annuity in its infancy. As consumers invested more and more money in these new products, asset managers, in turn, had to decide how to invest the funds. While the concept of annuity investment management is covered thoroughly in Chapter 10, we mention it here because it represents one of the main reasons for the fall of Baldwin-United. Baldwin-United chose to invest primarily in its own subsidiaries, using contractholders' annuity deposits to build the company. That practice has since been severely limited by state insurance departments.

By investing in its subsidiaries (affiliates), Baldwin had better control over its business/assets. However, investment in affiliates can also result in less liquidity should the parent company need to sell assets to cover liquidations. That's exactly what happened with Baldwin-United.

During the early part of 1981, Baldwin invested heavily in long-term bonds to match its annuity sales. Unfortunately, interest rates moved up sharply later that year, resulting in high annuity surrenders. Because interest rates were up, Baldwin was faced with liquidating bonds at a significant loss or trying to sell affiliated assets that were not particularly liquid.

To the extent that it could, Baldwin paid claims using surplus, annuity premiums and other revenue. However, this left the company deprived of cash that it needed to satisfy the huge debt incurred through its strategy of investing in affiliates. As the press focused on this debt issue, the value of Baldwin and its affiliates plunged, intensifying the problem. Finally, the state had to step in and, to protect contractholders, placed the company into receivership.

### The Fall of Charter Security

Charter Security failed under a completely different set of circumstances. Charter Security was owned by Charter Oil, one of the major players in the petroleum markets. Charter Oil went into bankruptcy because of the oil crisis of the early 1980s. To protect contractholders, the state came in and took over Charter Security to keep the parent company from draining money from its healthy insurance subsidiary.

### Other Scares

The annuity marketplace reinvented itself after a series of tax law changes during the 1980s. By the early 1990s, annuity sales were enjoying a nice run. Two of the largest underwriters of fixed annuities were Executive Life and the life companies of First Capital Holding. It would not be an exaggeration to say that these companies were run by aggressive management teams that wanted to keep their production sources satisfied. To that end, in response to their producers' insistence on higher yields and aggressive contract features, these companies began to invest heavily in lower quality bonds and untested derivatives in an effort to satisfy the demands of their market. Over time, the percentage of junk bonds in these carriers' portfolios grew to 50 percent, then 60 percent and eventually as high as 65 percent of company assets.

The fixed annuity is a product sold to individuals who are risk adverse and are looking for a safe and fair interest rate on their money as they save for retirement. Most experts in the field of annuities (including this text's authors) feel that junk bonds should never have exceeded 20 percent of the companies' portfolios, much less 65 percent. As a result of this exposure and the temporary paper losses associated with rising interest rates and their impact on all bonds, the insurance commissioners in the states of California and Virginia interceded on behalf of policyholders and liquidated the companies. Policyholders' contracts were either exchanged or liquidated, based on the desire of the policyholder. While most received 100 percent of their account balances, some owners of Executive Life contracts received less than 100 percent of their contracts' values.

### Industry Response

Following the Baldwin-United and Charter experiences in the 1980s, strict reinsurance, investment and accounting procedures relative to annuity products were put into place by the states. (The contractholders of Baldwin-United and Charter Security received all of their principal and a very reasonable interest rate on their funds through a rehabilitation effort led by Metropolitan Life.) The insurance company failures in the early 1990s again brought the annuity and concern for its safety into the spotlight. But again, lessons were certainly learned—the most significant being the need to limit junk bond investments as well as the importance of asset-liability matching, discussed in Chapter 10.

The insurance industry now has a better understanding of the liquidity that needs to be maintained in the annuity contract. The industry is in a better position to match investments with annuity contracts, which, as you will see, is the process of asset-liability matching. The variety of investment vehicles that exist in today's markets makes it more crucial than ever for insurance carriers to manage their annuity business efficiently and effectively.

## ■ DISTRIBUTION GROWTH

The significant growth in annuities during the mid- to late-1980s was, in part, a result of improved product design, but primarily resulted from expanded distribution. In addition to stockbrokers and insurance agents, two new distribution systems emerged: NASD broker-dealers and financial institutions. These two new distribution systems helped pave the way toward even wider consumer acceptance of the annuity product.

### Distribution Through NASD Broker-Dealers

While the NASD has existed since 1939, it has only been in the past 10 years or so that the smaller NASD broker-dealers have been organized enough to make significant inroads into insurance and annuity product distribution. Most of these NASD broker-dealers are loosely knit groups of financial planners, bound by a common service center that supports their business.

The basic financial planning skills that enable them to be successful in annuity sales have always existed among these individually registered representatives. However, it has taken the newly found marketing skills and organization of the broker-dealers to position annuities in such a fashion that they have become the day-to-day tool of the financial planner.

Though the distinction may be a subtle one, there is a difference between sales and marketing. The wire houses and insurance companies have done an exceptional job of training their sales representatives to be good salespeople. However, marketing and product positioning did not develop until the broker-dealers began to identify the annuity as a financial planning tool.

It was really the growth of individual financial planning that helped to build both the broker-dealer community and the annuity market. Stockbrokers became disenchanted with their corporate structure as commissions on annuities, mutual funds and limited partnerships were reduced significantly. Insurance professionals became disheartened as their home offices lagged in providing them with the much needed computer assistance necessary to provide the consumer with a complete and unbiased financial plan.

The solution became the independent broker-dealers. The broker-dealers provided the stockbroker and insurance professional alike with a comfortable base from which to do business. The sales professional, whether stockbroker or insurance agent, would give up the name recognition of the large stock exchange firm or insurance company affiliation and in return would receive higher commissions and access to a wider range of products and companies. For the annuity product and annuity carriers, this was good news. It represented broader distribution and better control over the ultimate client.

## Distribution Through Financial Institutions

When the first stockbroker sold the first deferred annuity in 1973, the lines that separated the various facets of the financial services industry began to fade. It would only be a matter of time before those lines became completely transparent and financial institutions entered the annuity market.

In 1983, savings and loans in California, Ohio, Florida and several other key states began selling annuities. The first major insurance company to offer annuity products through banks and savings and loans was a new company, founded in 1980, called Great Northern Annuity (GNA). Great Northern Annuity aggressively pursued the annuity market by offering to dedicate hundreds of thousands of dollars to advertising and promotion. In return, financial institutions agreed to sign a multiple-year exclusive contract with GNA. That was the birth of large-scale annuity marketing in financial institutions, even though there were other smaller scale projects that had started in other parts of the country.

The advent of financial institutions, such as banks and savings and loans, marketing annuities has forever changed the scope and the direction of the annuity market. Initial product offerings were not very consumer oriented, partly because of the higher commissions required to develop this new market. The products tended to be short on guarantees, long on surrender charges and heavy with commissions. However, as the 1990s began to unfold, the annuity products offered by institutions became

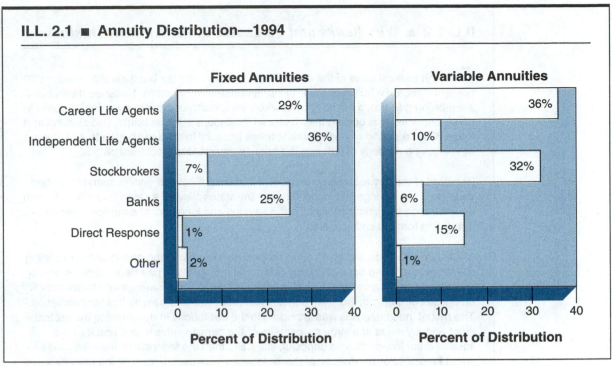

**ILL. 2.1 ■ Annuity Distribution—1994**

Fixed Annuities
- Career Life Agents: 29%
- Independent Life Agents: 36%
- Stockbrokers: 7%
- Banks: 25%
- Direct Response: 1%
- Other: 2%

Percent of Distribution

Variable Annuities
- Career Life Agents: 36%
- Independent Life Agents: 10%
- Stockbrokers: 32%
- Banks: 6%
- Direct Response: 15%
- Other: 1%

Percent of Distribution

Source: LIMRA

increasingly more competitive as demanded by both the consumer and the distributors.

Ultimately, financial institutions have created a healthy environment for the sale of the annuity. The promotion of annuity products by these institutions has elevated consumer awareness of annuities to an all-time high, making it easier for everyone to market annuities. Illustration 2.1 shows how annuities are distributed by channel of distribution.

## The Battle Between Agents and Banks

As banks have captured more and more of the annuity market, independent agents and insurance carriers that support agent distribution have put up a fight. They have taken their battle to each state that has legislation pending which would allow banks to sell annuity contracts. Agents argue that if banks are given the right to sell annuity contracts, undue pressure (such as credit tie-ins) could be brought to bear on the consumer to urge him or her to conduct annuity business with the bank. Banks counter that they have the legal right to sell annuities, a right that has been sanctioned by the Office of the Comptroller of the Currency, by states that have passed legislation allowing banks to own or operate insurance agencies and by the Supreme Court. In this regard, two high court cases are worth mentioning: *Variable Annuity Life Insurance Company v. NationsBank* and *Barnett v. Nelson*.

On January 18, 1995, the U.S. Supreme Court handed down what has come to be known as the VALIC decision. In this case, the Court ruled in favor of NationsBank

### ILL. 2.2  ■  *Why Banks and S&Ls Are in the Annuity Business*

The high interest rates of the early 1980s, coupled with tax brackets that reached 70 percent, created a bull market for the sale of deferred annuities. Because these sales were being generated primarily by stockbrokers, much of the money being invested in these annuities was coming from financial institutions such as banks and savings and loans. Over a period of several years, these financial institutions began to look toward developing a strategy of entering the annuity market to protect their profits.

Because of the regulatory environment at that time, most of the initial marketing efforts were made by savings and loans. Since many states allowed a savings and loan to own an insurance marketing subsidiary, the savings and loans could establish their own marketing force to sell annuities.

Initially, the savings and loans directed their annuity marketing efforts at their existing client base, with the hope of getting additional money from their depositors. However, these early days saw as much as 60 percent to 70 percent of savings and loans' annuity business coming from their own deposit accounts. This is known as "disintermediation." The mix of these deposits was important to the institutions in determining the profitability of annuity sales. If a large percentage of the annuity sales was a result of the liquidation of low-profit time deposits, like CDs, then the fee income from annuities could favorably offset the loss of those deposits. However, if most of the annuity sales were a result of depositors liquidating low-yield, high-profit savings accounts, then the institutions would have to reevaluate their marketing programs.

Today, the broader definition of financial institutions applies to banks, savings and loans and credit unions. In selling annuities, their position has shifted somewhat. From a defensive posture as described above, they're now on the offensive, using both the fixed and variable annuity as a springboard to other consumer investment products, such as mutual funds. In some cases, the reverse has been true, where a sophisticated broker-dealer distribution system at a bank has resulted in an expanded annuity effort. Annuity compensation plans have changed as well, allowing the institution to be paid with asset trails in return for a lower upfront commission.

One final note on the growth of annuity sales in the savings and loan market: When the FSLIC became bankrupt and the Resolution Trust Corporation was created, new rules were imposed on savings and loans. One requires that a savings and loan have a certain *capitalization ratio* (the ratio of tangible capital to deposits). This requirement has forced these institutions either to raise capital or shed deposits. Many institutions elected to move these core deposits into annuities. By doing so, the institutions have reduced their deposit base, increasing their capital to deposit ratio, and generated fee income from the sale of annuities.

in a suit brought by Variable Annuity Life Insurance Company (VALIC), which had argued that the annuity contract is not an investment contract, but rather an insurance contract that should be so treated under the insurance laws of the state. The Court disagreed, ruling that the annuity contract is an investment and that banks have the right to market investment products under national banking laws.

In late 1995, the Supreme Court ruled again, this time in *Barnett v. Nelson*. In this case, the Supreme Court reversed a lower court ruling. The lower court had found in favor of the state of Florida, which did not allow the sale of annuities or life insurance by banks in towns with populations of 5,000 or less. The state's position was contrary to the language found in Section 92 of the National Bank Act. In its unanimous decision to reverse the lower court, the Supreme Court ruled decisively that the National Bank Act preempts the state law prohibiting the sale of these products.

The insurance community, not satisfied with the Supreme Court decisions, has enjoined the battle elsewhere, lobbying Congress to change the Glass-Steagall Act, which separates banking and securities activities. Agents and their attorneys are arguing that Glass-Steagall should be modified to prohibit any further escalation in bank insurance powers. Another proposed amendment seeks to ensure that the states dictate the enforcement of insurance laws, thereby allowing states that do not want annuities sold by banks to continue to enforce their own laws. In many states, banks must still use the services of third-party marketing firms to sell their products.

As you can see, the issue of banks selling annuities is a complex one, crossing both state and federal lines. Not only is it an issue of who can sell these products, but who will regulate those sales—the state Departments of Insurance or the federal Office of the Comptroller of the Currency. It would appear that banks have made significant inroads in defining their right to sell annuities and in proving their capabilities to do so successfully. In 1995, despite several very restrictive states, banks accounted for 30 percent of all annuity sales.

Ultimately, banks have created a healthy environment for the sale of the annuity. The promotion of annuity products by these institutions has elevated consumer awareness of annuities to an all-time high, making it easier for everyone to market these products.


## ■ SUMMARY

In this chapter we reviewed the different distribution systems for the annuity and took a quick retrospective look at how the market developed. As with any industry, one must be able to look at the mistakes that were made and be able to say that something was learned from those mistakes. Undoubtedly, the insurance industry has learned a lot from its individual failures as well as the people who have sold these products. In today's annuity environment, insurance companies must be as comfortable with the distribution system as they are with the dynamics of the products.

The role of banks in the distribution of annuity products continues to develop. Many insurance industry experts feel that banks will expand, not contract, the market. These individuals argue that banks bring additional credibility to the annuity product, thereby making it easier for any licensed sales representative to sell the product. Bank promotional activity has also served to make the consumer more knowledgeable of and receptive to annuity products.

## ■ CHAPTER 2 QUESTIONS FOR REVIEW

1. Until the early 1970s, an annuity was normally used as an accumulation vehicle.

   *True* or *False*

2. Early annuity product design (mid-1970s) often contained bailouts and limited surrender charges.

   *True* or *False*

3. First in, first out (FIFO) treatment once granted to annuities was lost as a result of the Tax Equity and Fiscal Responsibility Act of 1982.

   *True* or *False*

4. Stockbrokers and insurance agents sought out broker-dealers to obtain more product diversity and financial independence.

   *True* or *False*

5. Which distribution source was responsible for the explosion of annuity sales in the late 1970s?

   a. Banks and savings and loans
   b. Insurance agents
   c. Stockbrokers
   d. Credit unions

# 3

# The Annuity as an Income Vehicle

I n Chapter 1 we discussed how annuities traditionally have been viewed and used as a vehicle to generate a fixed income stream for an individual. Immediate fixed annuities are specifically designed for this application. Prior to the early 1970s, immediate fixed annuities accounted for well over 90 percent of annuity sales. Today, they account for less than 20 percent. Why this dramatic change? There are three reasons:

1. The volatile interest rate environment since the early 1970s, which created a higher level of awareness among consumers as to the need for safe, tax-deferred accumulation and growth.

2. The rising popularity of a flexible alternative to an annuitized income stream, called "systematic withdrawal." Systematic withdrawal, an option available with deferred annuities, can also be used for income.

3. The growth of variable annuitization as an income option. With the explosive growth in variable annuities, several annuity carriers have specifically identified variable annuitization as an option for those individuals who want a guarantee, but who also have the risk tolerance to invest some portion of their annuity assets in a market value account.

In this chapter, we will look at the different ways that annuities are used to distribute income. We'll begin with the traditional approaches, examine their advantages and disadvantages, then move on to some of the newer, more flexible alternatives.

■ ■ ■ ■ ■

## ■ ANNUITY INCOME

The origin of the annuity is based on a fairly simple mathematical concept: a lump sum of money, invested today at a certain rate of interest, can be converted or "annuitized" into a series of periodic payments, calculated to extend for a specific period of time. The basic factors are *principal, interest* and *time*. Each periodic payment consists partly of amortized principal and partly of interest earnings.

What the insurance industry brought to the annuity equation was an added dimension that enabled annuity payments to be made for the duration of an individual's *life*. Because of their experience with mortality, insurers were qualified to combine this factor into the basic annuity calculation. This factor, in concept, is the same as a mortality factor in a life insurance premium calculation. Thus, it provides insurers with the means to make and guarantee annuity payments for life, regardless of how long that life lasts.

Any kind of annuity can be used to produce an income stream. An immediate annuity, by design, does so within a very short time—usually within one month of purchase, but never any later than 13 months. Deferred annuities, which accumulate their funds over time, can be annuitized (i.e., converted to an income stream) after any number of years. If the income stream is generated from a fixed annuity, the payments are definite and unchanging; if the income stream is generated from the separate account of a variable annuity, the income payments will fluctuate in response to the investment performance of the underlying funds.

For purposes of using the annuity to provide income, we can think of immediate annuities and annuitization as one. Creating an income stream with an immediate annuity is done through the purchase of an immediate annuity product, while an income stream from a deferred annuity is the result of annuitizing the product—that is, converting the accumulated amount in the deferred annuity into a flow of income. In either case, the objective is the same: to exchange a known sum of money today for a series of guaranteed payments over a period of time, usually a lifetime.

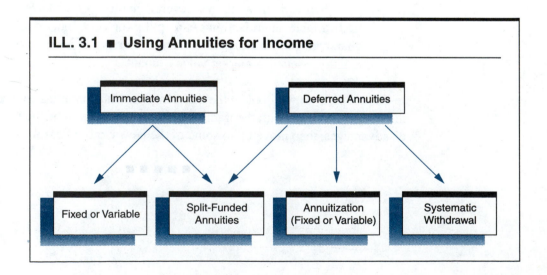

### ILL. 3.1 ■ Using Annuities for Income

It is easy to see how annuities can play an important role in any situation where a stream of income is needed, such as during retirement. The guarantee that the income will be paid for a specified period of time—or the guarantee that an individual cannot outlive the income payments—has brought peace of mind to countless numbers of people over the years. We will discuss the many ways in which an annuity income flow can be structured; however, let's first take a look at the factors that affect and determine the ultimate annuity benefit.

### Annuity Benefit Factors

When an annuity contractholder selects an income payout option, the insurance company must evaluate a number of factors before being able to arrive at a dollar amount for that specific option. The factors that the insurance company will look at include:

- the amount of the account being used to create the income stream;

- the investment environment at the time of the income election;

- assumptions on the reinvestment of cash flows for the insurer;

- assumptions on costs such as commissions, premium taxes, investment costs, etc.;

- the insurer's investment philosophy;

- the length of the payout desired (whether for a specified number of years or for life); and

- the number of lives covered (single vs. joint) and their ages and sex.

### ■ TRADITIONAL ANNUITY PAYOUT OPTIONS

To see how the above factors can influence the annuity and its income stream to the annuitant, let's look at an example. Assume Henry has $100,000 that he wants to use to purchase an immediate annuity. However, he is not sure which annuity payout option he should select. We will also assume that Henry is 60 years old and that his wife, June, is also 60. Following is an overview of the annuity options available to Henry (and June, where applicable), and the approximate amount of income that they would derive from those options.

### Life-Only Option

The *life-only* option represents the purest form of annuitization. It provides a series of guaranteed periodic payments (monthly, quarterly, semiannually or annually) for as long as the annuitant lives. When death occurs, payments stop. If there is any principal remaining that has not been paid out at the annuitant's death, it is forfeited. On the other hand, if the individual were to live forever, payments would continue forever.

Relative to payout options based on a life contingency, the life-only option produces the largest amount of income per dollar of principal. For Henry and his $100,000 premium, a life-only annuity option would produce $789 of income per month for the rest of his life.

## Life with Guaranteed Minimum Option

Although the life-only option provides a relatively large income stream, the fact remains that the principal amount is at risk should the annuitant die prior to receiving annuity payments equal to the premiums deposited. For this reason, insurers offer income options that guarantee a certain minimum amount of benefits. This guarantee can take the form of a certain number of benefit payments (a *life with term certain* payout) or one that promises to return all or a portion of the amount that the contractholder paid into the annuity (a *life with installment refund* or *cash refund* payout).

### Life with Term Certain

This option guarantees benefit payments for a specific number of years, whether the annuitant lives or dies, with payments guaranteed for life if the annuitant lives beyond that specified period. For example, a life with 10-year certain option would provide payments for life, and guaranteed for 10 years. If death occurs after 10 years, payments cease at death. If death occurs prior to 10 years, payments continue to the beneficiary for the remainder of the 10 years.

The term certain option is usually available for periods of 5, 10, 15 or 20 years. The longer the guaranteed period, the smaller the amount of each benefit payment. Should Henry select a life with 10-year certain payout, his monthly benefit would be $737.

### Life with Refund

This option is designed to guarantee the return or refund of the annuity's principal if the annuitant dies before the amount he or she paid into the contract is fully liquidated. It can take two forms: *installment refund* or *cash refund*. Under a life with installment refund, the annuitant receives periodic payments for life, with payments continuing to a beneficiary until the annuity's principal has been completely paid out. A life with cash refund payout would also make payments to the annuitant for life; however, if death occurs before the principal is depleted, the beneficiary would receive a lump-sum amount equal to any principal remaining. Keep in mind that, under either option, if the annuitant lives to receive payments equal to the principal amount, no future payments will be made to a beneficiary. An installment refund option would generate $714 a month for Henry; a cash refund option would produce $723 monthly.

## Joint-Life Options

All of the payout options just described are based on a single life. However, annuities can and often do provide income for two people. Here are Henry's options if he chooses to include June in the equation.

### Pure Joint Life

A *pure joint-life* payout option provides a specified income amount for two people, with payments stopping at the death of the first to die. As one might imagine, this type of payout option has a very limited appeal and is rarely used.

### Joint-Life and Survivor

A *joint-life and survivor* payout option provides income payments that continue as long as either of the two individuals is living, ceasing upon the death of the second individual. There are a number of ways in which this option can be arranged. For example, a *joint-life and 100 percent survivor* payout would provide a certain income benefit to both individuals and, at the death of the first, would continue the same payments to the survivor as long as he or she lives. A *joint-life and 50 percent survivor* payout would provide income payments to two people and, upon the death of the first, would make payments to the survivor equal to *half* the amount of the initial payments, as long as the survivor lives. For Henry and June, a joint-life and 100 percent survivor option would yield $664 per month whether one or both are alive. A joint-life and 50 percent survivor option would generate $708 per month while both are living.

A joint-life and survivor option can also incorporate a term certain guarantee. For example, a joint-life and survivor payout with a 10-year certain option would provide income payments to two individuals and guarantee that if both deaths occur within the first 10 years, payments will continue to a named beneficiary for the remainder of the 10 years.

## Term Certain Option

A *term certain* annuitization option is not based on a life contingency but simply guarantees payments for a specified number of years, such as 5 or 10. (Five years is usually the minimum.) Thus, the annuitant (or his or her named beneficiary) will receive an income stream for the selected period of time, regardless of whether the annuitant lives or dies. A 5-year term certain option would result in a monthly payment of $1,802 to Henry; a 10-year certain option would provide $1,077 monthly.

Practically speaking, the most common choices for payout options are life-only, life with term certain, joint-life and survivor and term certain. Illustration 3.2 shows how

## ILL. 3.2 ■ *Annuitization Payout Options*

The following illustrates the different benefit payments that a $100,000 annuity fund would generate, depending on the payout option selected. As you can see, the more "guarantees" the option provides, the smaller the monthly payment.

| Payout Option | Amount of Monthly Payment* |
|---|---|
| Life only | $789 |
| Life only with 10-year certain | $737 |
| Joint life and 50 percent survivor | $708 |
| Joint life and 100 percent survivor | $664 |
| Joint life and 50 percent survivor with 10-year certain | $698 |
| Joint life and 100 percent survivor with 10-year certain | $663 |
| Five-year certain | $1,802 |
| 10-year certain | $1,077 |

*Assumes the annuitant is a male, age 60, and his spouse/survivor is also age 60. The annuitant's life expectancy is 17.5 years; joint life expectancy is 25.7 years.

these options apply for Henry and June. Illustration 3.3 notes the rate of return for each option, based upon Henry's life expectancy (17.5 years) and Henry and June's joint-life expectancy (25.7 years). These returns are typically not high, and demonstrate the lack of inflation protection from a traditional fixed annuitization option. Illustration 3.3 also compares the rates of return for these same payout options, if Henry and June were to die 10 years prior to or 10 years after life expectancy. Note that there is a significant rate of return impact if death occurs prior to life expectancy. However, living beyond life expectancy will greatly increase the rate of return. As you might expect, the rates of return on term certain annuities are not affected by life expectancy variations.

## Taxation of Annuity Income Payments

Annuitized income payments are taxed according to a concept known as the *exclusion ratio*. Part of each payment the annuitant receives is considered to be a return of principal, which is not taxed. The remaining portion of the payment consists of interest earnings and is taxable to the annuitant. The exclusion ratio determines the taxable and nontaxable portions of each payment. Its formula is:

$$\frac{\text{Investment in the Contract}}{\text{Expected Return}}$$

**ILL. 3.3 ■ *Rates of Return on Annuitized Income Based on Life Expectancy***

The following shows the rates of return that each payout option from a $100,000 annuity provides, based on variances in life expectancy. As you can see, there is a significant rate of return impact if the annuitant and his or her survivor were to die prior to life expectancy. These returns are increased if the annuitant and his or her survivor were to live beyond life expectancy.

| Payout Option | Amount of Monthly Payment | Life Expectancy Rate of Return* | Death Occurs 10 Years Prior to Life Expectancy Rate of Return* | Death Occurs 10 Years After Life Expectancy Rate of Return* |
|---|---|---|---|---|
| Life only | $789 | 6.3% | − 8.8% | 8.5% |
| Life only with 10-year certain | $737 | 5.3% | − 2.4% | 7.8% |
| Joint life and 50 percent survivor | $708 | 7.1% | 3.8% | 8.0% |
| Joint life and 100 percent survivor | $664 | 6.4% | 2.9% | 7.4% |
| Joint life and 50 percent survivor with 10-year certain | $698 | 6.9% | 3.6% | 7.8% |
| Joint life and 100 percent survivor with 10-year certain | $663 | 6.4% | 2.9% | 7.3% |
| Five-year certain | $1,802 | 3.1% | 3.1% | 3.1% |
| 10-year certain | $1,077 | 5.3% | 5.3% | 5.3% |

*Assumes the annuitant is a male, age 60, and his spouse/survivor is also age 60. The annuitant's life expectancy is 17.5 years; joint life expectancy is 25.7 years.

The "investment in the contract" is the amount the annuitant paid into the annuity in the form of premiums; this is also known as the annuitant's "basis." The "expected return" is the total amount he or she will receive as income payments, based on the income option selected. The resulting ratio is the percentage of each benefit payment that is excluded from tax.

For example, assume Henry decides on a 10-year certain payout for his $100,000 annuity. As Ill. 3.2 shows, this option will generate $1,077 a month over the 10 years, or a total of $129,240. To determine the exclusion ratio, we divide Henry's basis in the contract—$100,000—by the expected return—$129,240. The result is 77.4 percent. This means that 77.4 percent of each $1,077 monthly payment, or $834, will be a tax-free return of principal and the remaining $243 will be taxed as interest earnings.

It should be noted that this discussion of the taxation of annuity income and the exclusion ratio applies to nonqualified annuities. The taxation of qualified annuity income is different because the premiums used to fund the qualified annuity may not have been taxed to begin with. A more thorough discussion of annuity taxation appears in Chapter 11.

## Advantages and Disadvantages of Fixed Annuitization

The advantage to a structured, guaranteed income flow is obvious: the annuitant is assured that the income will be paid for the duration of the specified period, whether it's a certain number of years or life. Each month or quarter or year, the insurer promises to make guaranteed payments of principal and interest to the annuitant. Some individuals, especially those in retirement, may be reluctant to use the principal of their savings, fearing it may become depleted. However, if they choose to conserve the principal, they run the risk of never deriving any benefit from it at all—and ultimately are obliged to pass it on to others at their deaths. A fixed annuity payout provides a certain, known income that will not change.

On the other hand, there are disadvantages to annuitization. For one thing, it is irrevocable. A fixed annuitized payout option commits the annuitant to an income flow and the methodical liquidation of his or her principal. Second, the rates of return on annuity income options are fixed at the time of purchase (immediate annuities) or at the point when the contract annuitizes (deferred annuities) and are typically not very high relative to current interest rates, as Ill. 3.3 shows. A fixed annuity payout has very little protection against inflation.

Finally, because the contractholder has converted his or her funds to a distribution mode, he or she has forfeited any rights to the underlying account balance. This means that the contractholder cannot change that income stream during life and his or her beneficiary receives no benefits from the insurer at the annuitant's death.

## ■ SYSTEMATIC WITHDRAWALS

From our discussion, it is apparent that in some circumstances the disadvantages of annuitization may outweigh the advantages. In recognition of this, the concept of *systematic withdrawal* was created in 1976 by SAFECO Life Insurance Company. Since that time, systematic withdrawal has become fairly commonplace in the nonqualified annuity market. Most annuity carriers today routinely offer systematic withdrawal as an income option or as a method of distributing the previous year's interest in the contract.

Systematic withdrawal is an alternative to an immediate annuity or annuitization, in that income is provided in the form of *withdrawals* from a deferred annuity. As you will learn, most deferred annuities allow for some level of annual withdrawals that are free of surrender charges. The typical annual withdrawal allowance is 10 percent

> ### ILL. 3.4 ■ *Commutable Annuities*
>
> **H**istorically, the decision to purchase an immediate annuity was irrevocable. Once a buyer elected to receive an annuitized income stream, that stream could not be altered or stopped. Obviously, this restricted the appeal of the product and, consequently, the market. Inflexible products have limited use.
>
> The first modern *commutable annuity* was introduced by Life of Virginia. This particular product gives the owner a certain period of time to commute the value of the contract into a lump sum. After that time, the contract locks in to an annuitized income flow for the term selected.
>
> The commutable contract represented a major breakthrough for the annuity as an income vehicle. Since its introduction, several other carriers have introduced competitive products that have built on the initial product design. The latest of these are a number of immediate variable annuities that offer the right to commute the contract's value into a single sum. For those who do not want to give up control of the money, these commutable annuities offer an advantage over the traditional immediate annuity.

of the annuity's accumulated value. The systematic withdrawal option takes this simple concept and expands it into a sophisticated method of distributing income to the contractholder. As with annuitization, payments are made on some regular (or systematic) basis. These payments are not tax advantaged; there is no exclusion ratio. In other words, all distributions are fully taxed until the earnings are gone, then, of course, recovery of basis is not taxable. Payments are also not guaranteed to last for a lifetime.

The major advantage of systematic withdrawal over annuitization is the flexibility it offers. The payments are completely and infinitely flexible. If income is not needed in a given year (or month) a withdrawal need not be taken. If more income is needed in a given year (or month) the contractholder may take more. Unlike annuitization that irrevocably commits principal to liquidation, the systematic withdrawal account balance is always available to the contractholder—a significant difference when compared to annuitization. Any monies that are in a contractholder's account at the time of death are payable to his or her beneficiary, bypassing probate. It is important to emphasize that none of the monies are forfeited to the insurance company—all go to the beneficiary.

The last big difference is inflation protection. Because the contractholder is not locked into an irrevocable, fixed payment schedule for life, the deferred annuity will continue to be credited with current interest each year. Therefore, at least theoretically, the credited rate should rise in some relation to the increase in market rates.

### Early Withdrawal Penalties

A final word about systematic withdrawals is in order. As you will learn in the next chapter and in Chapter 11, withdrawals from annuities may be subject to a 10 percent "early withdrawal" penalty if they are taken before the contractholder's age 59½. This penalty is applicable to systematic withdrawals, too, unless they are structured to conform to a prescribed amortization schedule set forth in the tax laws. Some companies have designed their systematic withdrawal programs to comply with these laws; others have not. It's important that the practitioner understand the potential penalty for his or her contractholders.

## ■ VARIABLE ANNUITIZATION

Fixed annuitization options and systematic withdrawals have their advantages; they also have disadvantages. A fixed annuitized income stream can be ravaged by inflation while systematic withdrawals, though flexible, do not offer effective long-term solutions to income needs. A better alternative, many contend, is *variable annuitization.*

Variable annuitization is nothing new. In many respects, the products being introduced today are not significantly different from the first variable annuitization product offered in 1952 by Teachers Insurance and Annuity Company (TIAC). Their concept was simple: income should be structured to meet the ever-present demon known as inflation. To address this ongoing need for greater levels of income, TIAC offered their annuitants the option of taking variable payments instead of fixed payments. The variable payments would fluctuate with the value of the underlying separate account assets which, in theory, would rise and fall in conjunction with consumer prices and changes in the cost of living. By linking the annuity payments to separate account investments, the annuitant's income would adjust for inflation, rising with increases in the cost of living and declining if and when prices fell. As it turned out, the concept more than lived up to expectations. For those TIAC annuitants who elected to take variable payments, their payment in 1992 was more than 10 times greater than their payment in 1952. Not bad, considering that the cost of living increased only four and a half times over that same period.

### The Mechanics of Variable Annuitization

Variable annuitization is accomplished by the contractholder selecting an *assumed investment rate* or *assumed interest rate* (AIR) and allocating the annuity fund to one or more separate account investment options. The insurance company then converts the amount of money in the contractholder's account into an initial payment, based on the AIR and payout period desired (term certain and/or life). The final step is to convert the initial payment into units based on the annuity unit value at the time of the first distribution. The resulting number of units is then used to calculate each future payment for the balance of the payout period or the term of the contract.

### The Assumed Interest Rate

The AIR is the rate of interest or the rate of investment growth that is assumed or projected for the contract's future performance. It is used as a benchmark against which the contract's actual return is measured. If the actual return exceeds the AIR, the annuitant realizes an increase in the payment amount. If the actual return is less than the AIR, the payment amount decreases. For example, assume a contract's AIR is 5 percent. If the accounts in which the contract's funds are invested increase at exactly 5 percent (net of mortality and expense charges), the annuity payment amount will remain level. If actual fund performance is less than 5 percent, the annuity payment amount will decrease; returns greater than 5 percent will lead to an increase in annuity payments.

Under most variable annuitization options, the contractholder selects the AIR, usually from among three or four different rates, typically ranging from 3.5 percent to 7 percent. Those who choose a higher AIR will initially receive a higher income than those who choose a lower rate. By the same token, the choice of a higher AIR will lead to a more rapid and precipitous drop in the payment amount if net returns are less than the assumed rate. Conversely, the choice of a lower AIR will start the payment level at a lower amount, providing something of a cushion against a declining market while at the same time making it more responsive to market increases. The following shows the difference between the initial annuity payment using three AIRs and based on a 65-year-old individual and a $100,000 annuity fund:

| AIR | Initial Monthly Payment |
|------|-------------------------|
| 3.5% | $666 |
| 5.0% | $763 |
| 7.0% | $899 |

As you can see, the lower the AIR, the lower the initial payment; the higher the AIR, the higher the initial payment. This serves as the benchmark going forward. For example, if the AIR is 5 percent and the account netted a constant 5 percent every year, the income payments to the annuitant would remain at $763 per month. If the account netted an interest rate higher than 5 percent, the payments would increase; if the account earned a rate lower than 5 percent, the payments would decrease. Illustration 3.5 shows how the monthly payments under various AIRs would change with a higher than assumed investment performance.

### Determining Initial and Subsequent Payments

Once the AIR has been determined, the insurer can establish the initial payment. This is done by applying a factor known as the *annuity purchase rate* to the account value. (Basically, the annuity purchase rate is the amount of income that each $1,000 of account value will provide, based on the assumed interest rate and the selected term.) In our example, the application of the annuity purchase rate to a $100,000 account, based on a 5 percent AIR, produces an initial payment of $763. At that point, the initial amount of $763 is converted into *annuity units* by dividing the initial payment amount by the current value of a single annuity unit. (See Ill. 3.6.) Assuming that the

---

### ILL. 3.5 ■ *Effect of Higher Than Assumed Return on Monthly Income*

The following table shows how actual returns that are higher than the AIR would affect distributions. Here, we're showing an actual gross return of 12 percent and an actual net return of 10.13 percent, after mortality and expense charges.

| AIR | Initial Monthly Distribution | Monthly Distributions at 12% Gross, 10.13% Net | | |
| --- | --- | --- | --- | --- |
| | | Year 2 | Year 10 | Year 20 |
| 3.5% | $666 | $708 | $1,239 | $2,304 |
| 5.0% | $763 | $800 | $1,229 | $1,980 |
| 7.0% | $899 | $926 | $1,200 | $1,600 |

---

annuity unit value is $10, the number of annuity units will be 76.3 ($763 ÷ $10). This number remains constant throughout the contract's distribution period. The units are revalued at each payment interval, reflecting the current market value of the underlying investments (as well as the insurer's mortality and expense experience). Consequently, each payment going forward will reflect 76.3 units multiplied by whatever the annuity unit value is.

If the annuity unit value increases at the same rate as the AIR, the distribution payments will remain level. Continuing with our example, as long as the annuity unit value increases at a net rate of 5 percent, the monthly payments would remain at $763. Net increases above 5 percent would produce payments greater than $763; growth of less than 5 percent would produce payments less than $763. Remember, once variable annuitization begins, the *number* of annuity units credited to the contract does not change; the insurer guarantees the payment of that unit quantity each

---

### ILL. 3.6 ■ *How Annuity Units Are Valued*

When an individual purchases a variable annuity, any amounts allocated to the separate account are converted from dollars into units. This is really no different from when a mutual fund converts investors' dollars into shares. The units represent the buyer's ownership of the particular subaccount or subaccounts invested in.

To determine the annuity unit value, the insurer takes the total value of the subaccount and deducts the cost of fund management as well as the mortality and expense charges detailed in the fund's prospectus. This amount is then divided by the contractholder's deposits. The result is the annuity unit value. This value is determined daily and will rise and fall based on the underlying performance of the account.

payment period for the duration of the payout term, however long that may be. What varies is the *level* of the payments, rising or falling in relation to the value of the annuity units.

### Picking an AIR

Given the significance of the AIR and how it affects future distributions, how does a contractholder go about selecting the AIR? A lower assumed rate, such as 3.5 percent, would most likely assure him or her of higher distributions in the future but will generate lower levels of income initially. (This should be pointed out to the client prior to annuitization: a lower assumed interest rate would require a larger premium deposit for the contract to generate the income necessary to meet the client's income goal.) On the other hand, selecting a higher AIR such as 7 percent will produce a high initial payment, but it establishes a more difficult benchmark for the contract's future performance. In fact, in many cases, a higher AIR virtually guarantees that the contractholder will receive smaller payments periodically. Illustration 3.7 shows what happens to our three illustrative annuity payments when the actual gross return is 4 percent and 1.93 percent after mortality and expense charges.

Which is better—a conservative AIR or a more aggressive projection? Like most investments, the answer depends on the contractholder's risk tolerance and his or her expectation for the future. A conservative investor will likely choose a lower AIR; those who want to start with as high a benefit amount as possible (and who believe future returns will match their optimism) usually opt for the higher AIR. Unless there are extenuating circumstances where the contractholder can adequately deal with the times his or her distributions will decrease, a conservative projection such as 4 percent or 5 percent is typically recommended.

---

### ILL. 3.7 ■ *Effect of Lower Than Assumed Return on Monthly Income*

The following table shows how an actual gross return of 4 percent (1.93 percent net after mortality and fund expenses) would change the monthly income payments for the various AIRs.

| AIR | Initial Monthly Distribution | Monthly Distributions at 4% Gross, 1.93% Net | | |
| --- | --- | --- | --- | --- |
| | | Year 2 | Year 3 | Year 4 |
| 3.5% | $666 | $656 | $572 | $491 |
| 5.0% | $763 | $741 | $567 | $422 |
| 7.0% | $899 | $857 | $554 | $341 |

### ILL. 3.8 ■ *Annuitization vs. Systematic Withdrawals*

| | Fixed Annuitization | Variable Annuitization | Systematic Withdrawal |
|---|---|---|---|
| Full Rights to Principal | NO | NO | YES |
| Inflation Protection | NO | YES | YES |
| Guarantee of Principal | MAYBE | MAYBE | YES |
| Preservation of Tax Deferral | YES | YES | YES |
| Full Options Available to Beneficiary | NO | NO | YES |
| Estate Preservation | MAYBE | MAYBE | YES |
| Liquidity | NO | NO | YES |
| Customized Income Flow | NO | NO | YES |
| Guaranteed Income for Life | YES | YES | NO |

## ■ SPLIT-FUNDED ANNUITIES

*Split-funded annuities* are a comparatively recent development, whereby an immediate annuity and a deferred annuity are combined to accomplish some specific financial objectives. These objectives are:

- conserving principal;

- maintaining flexibility;

- receiving income; and

- providing tax advantages.

Often individuals will not want to commit to a lifetime payout option. They may only wish to take income for a period of time, then reevaluate their economic situation, their risk tolerance and the economic conditions in general. Obviously a traditional immediate annuity does not provide this flexibility. Illustration 3.9 illustrates how a split-funded annuity meets these objectives.

Basically, contractholders take their initial premium and "split" it into two contracts, one a deferred annuity and the other an immediate annuity. The purpose of the deferred portion is to preserve principal. This is done by locking in a guaranteed interest rate for a period of time matching the immediate annuity payout period. The amount deposited into the deferred annuity is determined by calculating how much is necessary to grow back to the initial total deposit at the guaranteed rate over the guarantee period.

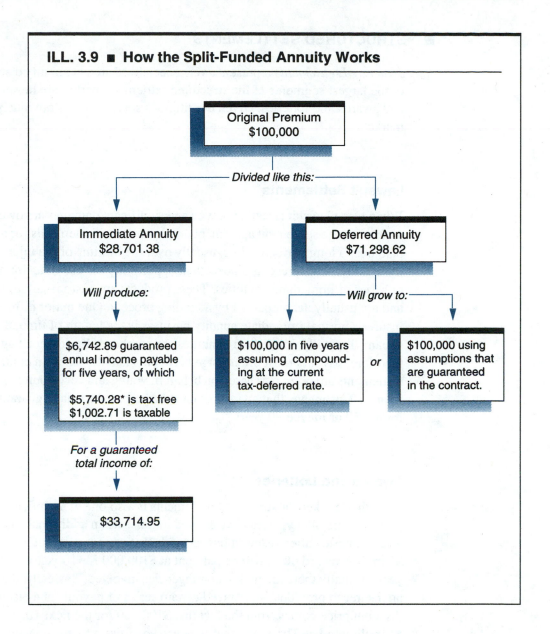

**ILL. 3.9 ■ How the Split-Funded Annuity Works**

Original Premium
$100,000

*Divided like this:*

Immediate Annuity
$28,701.38

Deferred Annuity
$71,298.62

*Will produce:*

*Will grow to:*

$6,742.89 guaranteed annual income payable for five years, of which

$5,740.28* is tax free
$1,002.71 is taxable

$100,000 in five years assuming compounding at the current tax-deferred rate.

*or*

$100,000 using assumptions that are guaranteed in the contract.

*For a guaranteed total income of:*

$33,714.95

The remaining amount of the initial deposit is then used to fund a term certain immediate annuity. The immediate annuity provides income for the stated period. As previously explained, the income is tax advantaged because part of each payment is considered to be a return of principal. (It is important to note again that the tax advantage applies only to nonqualified monies, not pensions, TSAs or IRAs. It is also important to note that subsequent splits will not enjoy the tax advantage of the exclusion ratio.)

At the end of the guarantee period, the contractholder has his or her entire principal and may choose to do anything he or she wishes at that point, while during the guarantee period, he or she was able to enjoy stable income in a tax-advantaged fashion.

## ■ STRUCTURED SETTLEMENTS

*Structured settlements* represent a very specialized area of annuity distributions. Two of the largest segments of the structured settlement market are lawsuit settlements and awards and lotteries. Given our litigious society, this is obviously a growing market.

### Lawsuit Settlements

Whenever a lawsuit is settled or won and significant damages are owed by one party to another, the settlement agreement or court mandate often calls for the money to be paid over a long period of time, usually over the lifetime of the injured party or family member. This presents an excellent opportunity for use of an immediate annuity or series of immediate annuities. These products are custom-tailored for each case and are usually accompanied by a bidding process. One major difference from an insurer's normal immediate annuity business is the length of time of the payout stream. Typically, immediate annuities are purchased by someone age 60 or older; therefore, payouts most often range between 5 and 30 years. In contrast, structured settlements are often purchased on behalf of young and very young individuals, even infants. This means that an insurer must be prepared to make guaranteed payments for 40, 50 or maybe 90 years.

### Awards and Lotteries

The other market for structured settlements is also one of significant growth. In the past 10 years, many states have created lotteries as an additional source of revenue. These lotteries often result in huge awards that are not paid out in a lump sum. A $1 million award often will be paid out at $100,000 for 10 years, or $50,000 for 20 years. Usually there are no life contingencies involved. Basically, the states look for an insurer to provide a guaranteed certain series of payouts at a discount price. The discount price comes from the fact that $100,000 for the next 10 years is not worth $1 million today. Therefore, that state can advertise a $1 million award and provide for this award with the purchase of a structured settlement from an insurance company for something less than $1 million.

## ■ SUMMARY

Just a few years ago, a discussion of using an annuity for income would have addressed only immediate annuities and fixed payout options. Like so many other aspects of annuities, however, things have changed. For the most part, these changes have been brought about by economic conditions and consumer demands. The demand for systematic withdrawal has grown exponentially in the last few years as consumers have demanded inflation protection, principal conservation and flexibility from their annuity payouts. This trend is expected to continue.

In addition, the growth of variable annuitization has been significant. Several annuity carriers have introduced special products geared specifically toward this concept. Over the coming years, we can expect to see more and more emphasis on asset allocation as it applies to the distribution side of the annuity equation, not just the accumulation side. This will result in insurers helping consumers choose between a mix of income options, balancing fixed and variable annuitization with systematic withdrawals to best meet their income needs.

## ■ CHAPTER 3 QUESTIONS FOR REVIEW

1. Deferred annuities cannot be used to generate income prior to annuitization.

   *True* or *False*

2. Split-funded annuities are often used to satisfy lawsuit settlements.

   *True* or *False*

3. The exclusion ratio determines

   a. the amount of annuity payout excluded from estate taxes.
   b. the amount of annuity payout excluded from ordinary income tax.
   c. the amount of annuity payout subject to capital gains treatment.
   d. None of the above

4. Which of the following annuity payout options would provide the best protection against inflation?

   a. Life-only immediate annuity
   b. Joint-life with 50 percent survivor immediate annuity
   c. Systematic withdrawal
   d. Ten-year term certain immediate annuity

5. If the contractholder desires maximum lifetime income now and has no heirs, the best payout option would be a

   a. life-only immediate annuity.
   b. joint-life with 50 percent survivor immediate annuity.
   c. systematic withdrawal.
   d. 10-year term certain immediate annuity.

6. Assuming an AIR of 5.0 percent and a one-year gross return of 5.0 percent on a variable annuitized account, the next schedule payout would

   a. increase.
   b. decrease.
   c. stay the same.

# 4

# The Annuity as an Accumulation Product

A nnuities come in all different shapes and sizes. Some are oriented to distribution; however, the vast majority are used to accumulate a sum of money for distribution at some point in the future, usually retirement. These are deferred annuities.

There are many different deferred annuity products (including variable deferred annuities), which we will discuss in the next few chapters. In this chapter, we will focus on the fixed deferred annuity and look at the features that are consistent from product to product. We will also cover the annuity contract and its provisions. As an added reference aid, a specimen policy appears in the Appendix. This specimen policy will give you some idea of the contract language found in a typical deferred annuity policy.

■ ■ ■ ■ ■

## ■ FEATURES OF FIXED DEFERRED ANNUITIES

This chapter focuses on the features of fixed deferred annuity products. We will look at how these annuities are purchased, common contract provisions, ways in which insurers assess surrender charges, methods of crediting annuity interest and ways in which contractholders can meet liquidity needs by accessing their annuity cash values during the deferral or accumulation period.

### Single Premium

Most of the annuity business written today as well as in the past has been *single premium* in nature. In a single-premium deferred annuity (SPDA), the contractholder makes one deposit at the beginning of the contract and is then prohibited from making subsequent deposits to that contract. Should he or she wish to make additional deposits, a second contract must be purchased. Obviously, when the individual purchases another contract, there is a new interest rate credited and a new and separate surrender charge schedule that applies to the new contract.

Typically, most insurance companies require a minimum deposit of $5,000 to purchase a single-premium annuity. Some companies will waive the $5,000 minimum if the deposit is being made as part of an IRA. In those cases, the minimum is usually $2,000, consistent with statutory IRA limits.

The advantage of purchasing an annuity through a single premium is that there are usually no administrative fees charged on the policy. Unlike the flexible premium annuity, discussed next, single-premium annuities require relatively little maintenance. As a matter of fact, because of size efficiencies, some insurance companies will actually give the contractholder an interest rate bonus for larger deposits.

## Flexible Premium

The major limitation of the single-premium annuity is that many people may not be able to deposit $5,000 at one time. For those individuals, the *flexible premium* deferred annuity (FPDA) is more convenient. The flexible premium annuity may require a minimum initial premium, such as $500 to $1,000, but will then most likely allow the contractholder to make additional deposits of as little as $25 to the contract, as frequently as he or she wishes. Many companies have even set up preauthorized contributions to their flexible premium annuity products by systematically transferring periodic sums from the contractholder's checking or savings account into the annuity.

There are many varieties of annuities that exist just for the flexible premium annuity buyer. Tax-sheltered annuities and IRA annuities are usually flexible premium contracts to allow monthly contributions to the employee's account or the individual's account. Credit unions, banks and savings and loans are beginning to market flexible premium annuities because of the demographics of their marketplace. These distributors tend to work with clients who may have difficulty meeting the large, single deposit required for the single-premium contract.

There are some drawbacks to the flexible premium annuity. The duration of surrender charges tends to be somewhat longer and the charges themselves somewhat higher. This is in part a result of additional administrative costs and the higher agent compensation typically found in flexible premium contracts. Flexible premium annuities may also carry annual policy fees or administration charges, which exist for a number of reasons. Obviously, the contractholder's right to make additional deposits requires the insurer to handle smaller amounts of money more frequently, which results in higher administrative costs. What may not be readily apparent is the additional cost of data processing support. The insurer must have systems support to handle the multiple deposits and must be able to track the various deposits for purposes of crediting initial and renewal interest rates.

As a final note, flexible premium annuities may also provide some degree of additional protection against future tax law changes. Congress has historically grandfathered any new legislation that adversely affects annuities. As such, a flexible premium annuity purchased prior to any adverse legislation may not be affected by the new law. This would enable the individual to continue to enjoy the tax benefits of the older policy while making additional contributions to the contract.

## Issue Ages

Deferred annuity *issue ages* are fairly standard, ranging from age 0 to 90, with most insurers issuing contracts without restrictions from age 0 to 75 and conditionally issuing contracts from age 76 to 90. Immediate annuities may be issued to individuals well into their 90s. At the older ages, deferred annuity contracts become very expensive for the insurance company; consequently, there are issue limitations at the older ages. (These restrictions will be discussed again briefly in Chapter 10, when we learn how insurers manage mortality risk.)

## Maturity Date

Every annuity contract will specify a *maturity date*. The maturity date, or "annuity date" as it's often called, is the date on which annuitized payments are scheduled to begin. The maturity date in most annuity contracts is the later of 10 contract years or the contract anniversary that falls in the year the annuitant reaches age 85. It should be noted, however, that most insurers will allow the contractholder/annuitant to continue the deferral period for some time past the maturity date.

Typically, most annuity contracts specify that the insurer has a right to require proof that the annuitant is living on the date of any annuity payment.

## Death Benefit Prior to Maturity

Most deferred annuity contracts provide for the payment of a *death benefit*. Some contracts provide for a death benefit in the event that either the annuitant or the contractholder (if different) dies before the maturity date. Other contracts provide for a death benefit only if the owner dies. The benefit is usually expressed as the amount of premiums paid, less any withdrawals, or the contract's accumulated value, if greater.

If death occurs after the contract's maturity date, payments will continue as provided for under the distribution option in effect.

### Free-Look Period

Just like life and health insurance contracts, all annuity contracts contain a *free-look provision,* which allows the buyer a period of 10 to 30 days after purchase to return the contract and receive a full refund of premiums paid. It should be noted that no interest is paid on the premium in the event the contractholder does return the contract for a refund.

### Misstatement of Age or Sex Provision

Also like life and health policies, annuity contracts include a clause that provides for a benefit adjustment if the age or sex of the annuitant is misstated in the application. This provision adjusts benefits to those that the premium would have purchased at the correct age or sex.

### Surrender Charges

Almost all deferred annuities have *surrender charges.* These charges are assessed during the early years of the contract should the contractholder liquidate or surrender the annuity before the insurer has had an opportunity to recover the cost of issuing the contract. In addition to recovering issuing costs, the surrender charges also provide some protection against *disintermediation.*

While discussed more thoroughly in Chapter 10, disintermediation is one of the primary risks that an insurance company assumes when managing annuity assets. Specifically, it is the risk that increasing interest rates will result in contractholders prematurely surrendering their annuity contracts, forcing the insurer to liquidate its underlying investments at an inappropriate time. Surrender charges help offset the potential loss in the insurer's portfolio if interest rates escalate after a contractholder purchases the annuity.

There are three ways insurers assess these surrender charges. Let's take a look.

#### Account Value or Premium Deposit Methods

The two most common ways of assessing surrender charges are both based on percentages. The *account value method* is based on a percentage of the full accumulated account value at the time of surrender, whereas the *premium deposit method* is based on a percentage of the premium or premiums that the contractholder has deposited into the contract. Illustration 4.1 shows the difference.

Annuity A uses the premium deposit method. As you can see, the surrender charge percentage is high in the initial years but reduces over time to zero in the eighth contract year. Annuity A applies the percentage only to the initial amount deposited in the contract, which is $100,000. Consequently, a complete surrender at the end of year one would result in a charge of $7,000. A complete surrender at the end of year five would result in a charge of $3,000.

## ILL. 4.1 ■ *Annuity Surrender Charges*

| | Annuity A (Premium Deposit Method) | Annuity B (Account Value Method) | Annuity C (Loss of Interest Method) |
|---|---|---|---|
| Surrender charges by year: | 7%, 6%, 5%, 4%, 3%, 2%, 1%, 0% | 4%, 4%, 4%, 4%, 4%, 4%, 0% | Six months' loss of interest |
| Basis of surrender charge: | Percentage of premium | Percentage of accumulated value | Annual interest |
| Amount of surrender charge: | | | |
| Year 1 | $7,000 | $4,320 | $4,000 |
| 2 | $6,000 | $4,666 | $4,320 |
| 3 | $5,000 | $5,039 | $4,666 |
| 4 | $4,000 | $5,442 | $5,039 |
| 5 | $3,000 | $5,877 | $5,442 |
| 6 | $2,000 | $6,348 | $5,878 |
| 7 | $1,000 | $0 | $0 |
| 8 + | $0 | | |

This example assumes an initial deposit of $100,000 and an 8 percent rate.

Using the account value method, Annuity B has surrender charges that disappear after six years, but the percentage is fixed at 4 percent and is assessed against the entire accumulated account. So, while a complete surrender at the end of year one would only result in a $4,320 surrender charge, a full surrender at the end of year five would result in a charge of $5,877. This information can be useful when comparing one contract to another.

### Loss of Interest

Recent years have seen the development of another method of assessing surrender charges, called *loss of interest*. With this type of surrender charge, the contractholder is penalized by a loss of interest over some period of time, usually six months to one year. Referring again to Ill. 4.1, we see that Annuity C has a surrender charge equal to six months' loss of interest. A complete surrender at the end of year one would result in a charge of $4,000. A complete surrender at the end of year five would result in a charge of $5,442. You will find loss of interest surrender charges on many of the certificate annuities. This is to create a closer parallel to a bank CD, which typically expresses premature withdrawal penalties as a loss of interest.

## ■ METHODS OF CREDITING ANNUITY INTEREST

There are numerous ways for insurance companies to invest annuity monies and credit interest to their contracts. In this section, we will focus on the three most popular methods:

1. new money rate;

2. portfolio rates; and

3. index interest rates.

Keep in mind that it is possible to combine some of these methods in limited ways. In addition, it is important to understand how the insurer is compounding the interest. In other words, is it compounded daily, monthly, quarterly or annually? The significance of compounding will be discussed in Chapter 8.

### Minimum Interest Rates

Before we look at the various ways insurers credit interest to their annuity contracts, it's important to emphasize that every fixed deferred annuity contract contains and guarantees a minimum interest rate. This minimum reflects, in part, the reserving and nonforfeiture requirements every insurer must meet. In effect, the minimum interest rate provides a "guaranteed, worst-case" scenario relative to interest rates. For most annuities, the minimum interest rate is 3 percent to 4 percent.

With some product designs, the minimum rate has little meaning. As you will learn, the certificate annuity, for example, always guarantees the current interest rate through the end of the surrender charge period. In these cases, the minimum interest rate would have little bearing on the contract from the contractholder's perspective.

With this introduction in mind, let's turn our attention to how insurers credit interest in excess of the minimum guaranteed rate, which, of course, is what interests the contractholder.

### New Money Rate

A *new money* method of crediting interest is sometimes referred to as "pocket" or "bucket" investing. In managing the new money interest rate, the insurer will place the annuity premium deposits during any given interest rate cycle into a pocket or bucket. Monies will be directed into the same bucket as long as interest rates remain relatively stable. It should be noted that in a period of widely fluctuating interest rates, an insurer may open and close a bucket in as short a period of time as one week. Once these buckets have been established, the insurer will evaluate each of them at renewal time to establish the renewal rate. The insurer will look at the cash flows from the underlying investments, reinvestment of the undistributed cash flows and the market value of the investment portfolio, as well as many other factors before arriving at a renewal rate.

It is important to understand that the declared renewal rate will be applicable only to those contracts issued during the time that the bucket was open. What this means is that each contractholder is, in essence, buying into a limited portfolio of investments available at that particular time. This is contrary to the portfolio rate method of investing, which we will discuss next.

A new money method is the most difficult way to credit and administer annuity interest. A year of heavily fluctuating interest rates will result in numerous buckets being created. So why do insurers use this method? Most experts agree that it is the fairest way to treat the contractholder and the safest way for the insurer to manage its annuity business. Should interest rates move up or down dramatically, the buckets are in a better position to react to those changes because of their structure.

## Portfolio Rates

By contrast, *portfolio rate* interest crediting is very simple to understand. All annuity monies go into one large pool or portfolio. The total return of that portfolio is used to establish the interest rate for all contractholders who buy that annuity. When it comes to renewal time, the insurer looks at the entire portfolio, regardless of when each individual investor bought his or her contract, and assigns a renewal rate for the entire block.

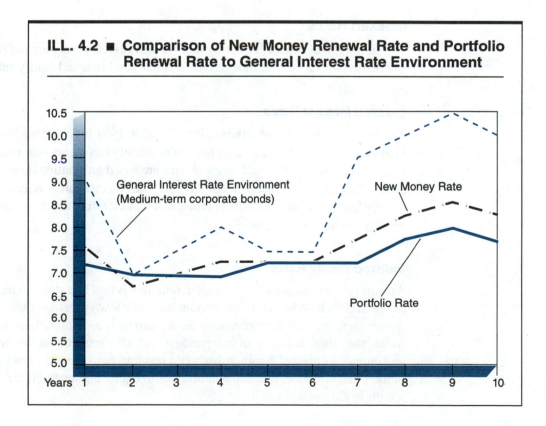

**ILL. 4.2 ■ Comparison of New Money Renewal Rate and Portfolio Renewal Rate to General Interest Rate Environment**

Portfolio rate annuities can also use different methods of declaring interest rates. Most portfolio rate insurers simply have one interest rate that is applied to all contractholders within the portfolio. A few insurers with portfolio rate annuities will credit interest on a calendar year basis. For example, let's say that Portfolio Life Insurance Company credits interest on a portfolio basis. Each year on January 15 the company sets the rate for the annuity block based on the entire portfolio. Regardless of when a contractholder deposits money with Portfolio Life, he or she will earn the interest rate declared until the following January 15. Most insurers have moved away from this method because of the obvious exposure to volatile interest rate movements.

Theoretically, portfolio rates are considered to be fair to contractholders because rates move up or down with equal probability and old and new contractholders share in these changes. There is a flaw in this theory, however, as shown in Ill. 4.3.

In the falling rate environment, this insurer would be crediting 6 percent to its contracts while comparable carriers credit 5 percent. This insurer then would either have all the business it wants or be able to achieve tremendous profits. The reverse is supposed to happen in the rising rate scenario, but it does not. This carrier is now forced to acquire new business at 6 percent when its competitors are offering 7 percent. Actually, the first dollar of new business will have to be acquired at 5 percent with competitors at 7 percent. This will *not* happen. To remain competitive, this carrier will have to close this portfolio and start anew. This means that old deposits *never* get the advantage of rising rates but *always* get the disadvantage of falling rates.

## Indexed Rates

The final type of interest crediting that we will review is an *indexed rate of return*. There are two variations: indexed interest rates and indexed equity rates.

### Indexed Interest Rates

The first indexed rate annuity was introduced in 1981 by National Home Life (now Providian Life and Health). This particular annuity has a one-year interest rate guarantee and subsequent annual renewal rates are based on a national independent bond index. By utilizing an independent measure, the contractholder is guaranteed that the insurer has no influence over the index and will therefore credit a competitive rate relative to the market.

### Indexed Equity Rates

An equity index annuity has a credited ratio that is tied to a stock market index, such as the S&P 500. Whereas virtually none existed a few years ago, these products have grown significantly; approximately 30 are currently available. Like the interest index, the return is tied to an independent, outside measure that the insurer does not and cannot influence. Again, this should result in fair renewal rates based on stock market performance. Indexed annuities, both equity and interest, are discussed at length in Chapters 5 and 9.

---

### ILL. 4.3 ■ *The Flaw in Portfolio Rate Interest Crediting*

---

| **In a Rising Rate Environment . . .** | | **In a Falling Rate Environment . . .** | |
|---|---|---|---|
| ***Initial Period*** | | ***Initial Period*** | |
| Market Rate | 7.0% | Market Rate | 9.0% |
| Initial Annuity Rate | 5.0% | Initial Annuity Rate | 7.0% |
| Competitor's Rate | 5.0% | Competitor's Rate | 7.0% |
| Sales | $100,000,000 | Sales | $100,000,000 |
| ***1 Year Later*** | | ***1 Year Later*** | |
| Market Rate | 9.0% | Market Rate | 7.0% |
| Annuity Rate* | 6.0% | Annuity Rate* | 6.0% |
| Competitor's Rate | 7.0% | Competitor's Rate | 5.0% |
| Company Sales | $100,000,000 | Company Sales | $100,000,000 |

*This is the renewal rate for existing business as well as the initial rate for new business; determined by weighting half the portfolio at 7 percent and half at 5 percent (5 percent derived from market rate minus spread).

*This is the renewal rate for existing business as well as the initial rate for new business; determined by weighting half the portfolio at 5 percent and half at 7 percent (7 percent derived from market rate minus spread).

In all the examples, the required spread difference between the market rate and the annuity rate is 2 percent.

## ■ DEFERRED ANNUITY LIQUIDITY OPTIONS

As we have learned, deferred annuity contractholders in the past had very few options in the event they wanted to or needed to access the cash values in their contracts. In fact, the earliest forms of the deferred annuity had no provision for cash benefits other than annuitization and later product generations offered contractholders little more than lump-sum distributions through complete surrenders (with possible exposure to surrender charges). Today, most deferred annuities provide some measure of liquidity so that, even during the deferral stage, contractholders can meet an emergency cash flow need. The two most popular forms of liquidity are the *free withdrawal* and the *policy loan*.

### Free Withdrawals

The *free withdrawal* was first introduced in the late 1970s to allay the liquidity fears that were being expressed by potential and existing contractholders. It is a provision that allows the contractholder to withdraw a stipulated amount from his or her annuity without incurring any surrender charges.

### ILL. 4.4 ■ *Free Withdrawals Before Surrender*

|  | Surrender Charge Without 10 Percent Free Withdrawal | Surrender Charge After Utilizing 10 Percent Free Withdrawal |
|---|---|---|
| Annuity with year four 4 percent surrender charge, crediting 8 percent interest; year four value = $136,048 | $5,442 | $4,898 |

The most common form of free withdrawal is the *10 percent free withdrawal*. It is usually offered after the first contract year for the remainder of the contract years during which a surrender charge applies. The withdrawal can be expressed as a percentage of the original premium deposit or as accumulated interest, but is most typically expressed as a percentage of the accumulated account value within the contract. Obviously, the more consumer-oriented contracts are those that base the withdrawal on the accumulated account value.

### Withdrawals Before Surrenders

One important potential benefit—or potential drawback—to a given annuity contract is the manner in which the insurer treats a full surrender. Some insurers automatically take the 10 percent free withdrawal prior to assessing any applicable penalties for a full surrender, if the contractholder had not used it. Others simply assess the full surrender charge and ignore the 10 percent free withdrawal. The difference between these two approaches is shown in Ill. 4.4. Applying the same assumptions we used to discuss policy surrender charges, we can see that by surrendering Annuity B at the end of the fourth year, after taking the 10 percent free withdrawal, the contractholder incurs a $4,898 surrender charge. If the insurer does not allow the 10 percent free withdrawal first, the surrender charge would increase to $5,442.

### Policy Loans

A second form of liquidity is available through *policy loans*. Policy loans on nonqualified annuities are a fairly recent development; in fact, prior to 1986, they did not exist. Initially offered in the TSA markets, policy loan provisions for nonqualified annuities were created as an alternative to the 10 percent free withdrawals. Policy loans in nonqualified annuities differ significantly from TSA loans in that a loan from a nonqualified annuity is taxable and, if taken before age 59½, can result in a premature distribution penalty as well. (See "Early Withdrawals and Taxes," later in this chapter.)

Interest is charged on policy loans and it is usually tied to independent indexes for purposes of establishing the amount. In a typical policy loan arrangement, the insurer

---

### ILL. 4.5 ■ *Policy Loan Provisions*

**P**rovisions for loans to contractholders are a fairly new development for nonqualified annuities. A typical loan provision would allow the contractholder to borrow up to 75 percent of the accumulated value in his or her account, at the following cost:

The higher of (a) the difference between the annuity's credited rate and Moody's AAA corporate bond index or (b) 1 percent.

**Example 1**

| | |
|---|---|
| Moody's AAA corporate bond index: | **9.0%** |
| Credited annuity rate: | **− 8.5%** |
| Difference: | **0.5%** |
| Cost charged to contractholder: | **1.0%** (contract minimum) |

**Example 2**

| | |
|---|---|
| Moody's AAA corporate bond index: | **10.0%** |
| Credited annuity rate: | **− 8.5%** |
| Difference: | **1.5%** |
| Cost charged to contractholder: | **1.5%** |

---

will allow the contractholder to borrow up to 75 percent of the accumulated account value. There is almost always a minimum interest charge to the contractholder. For example, the insurer might charge the difference between the credited rate on the contract and the current rate on the Moody's AAA corporate bond index, with a minimum charge of 1 percent. Illustration 4.5 shows how an indexed loan might work.

### Nursing Home, Hospitalization and Terminal Illness Provisions

The final means of annuity liquidity that we will cover is relatively new to the industry and deals specifically with annuitants or contractholders who are confined to a nursing home or hospital or are diagnosed as terminally ill. Several insurance carriers have developed provisions for their annuities that allow those who qualify to withdraw all or some of their money should they meet the standard criteria.

These new provisions are still being developed and refined. Each carrier treats this form of liquidity differently, so a careful review of each contract's provision is mandatory. There can be severe limitations that can mitigate the benefits. For example, if the withdrawal privilege is not exercised within a certain time period after admittance to a nursing home or hospital, it may be lost.

### Early Withdrawals and Taxes

The fact that today's deferred contractholders can more easily access their contract values may be somewhat overshadowed by the possibility that there could be significant tax consequences for doing so.

Before the passage of the Tax Equity and Fiscal Responsibility Act of 1982 (TEFRA), annuity distributions prior to age 59½ were not penalized. The effect of TEFRA was to assess a 5 percent penalty to annuity distributions attributed to interest earnings and taken before age 59½. The Tax Reform Act of 1986 increased the 5 percent penalty to 10 percent, where it remains today.

This 10 percent penalty is assessed only on interest earned and withdrawn, not on any principal that may have been withdrawn. In addition, this penalty can be avoided at any time by annuitizing with a life contingency or by using certain types of systematic withdrawals.

## ■ PREMIUM TAXES

A *premium tax* is a separate tax levied on life insurance and/or annuity premiums by individual states. Illustration 4.6 shows which states currently impose premium taxes. Note that most states that have premium taxes differentiate between qualified and nonqualified premiums. Depending on the state, premium taxes may be assessed differently.

The significance of premium taxes to contractholders is that they ultimately bear the cost. The method of assessing premium taxes should be covered in the annuity contract. It may also be explained in the sales literature the insurer uses.

## ■ ANNUAL STATEMENT

All insurance companies provide their contractholders with annual statements that contain basic information relative to account values and transactions. Some insurers prepare this accounting at the end of each contract year and some do so at the end of each calendar year. Regardless of when the statement is prepared, it provides information on all activity within that account during the year.

These statements are usually easy to read and understand. Even if the method of crediting interest is the new money method, which, as discussed, could contain

## ILL. 4.6 ■ *State Premium Taxes*

Many states impose a tax on annuities, assessed against premiums deposited or the accumulated value.

| State | Tax Rate Qualified Contracts | Nonqualified Contracts |
|---|---|---|
| California | .50% | 2.35% |
| District of Columbia | 2.25% | 2.25% |
| Kansas | .00% | 2.00% |
| Kentucky | 2.00% | 2.00% |
| Maine | .00% | 2.00% |
| Nevada | .00% | 3.50% |
| South Dakota | .00% | 1.25% |
| West Virginia | 1.00% | 1.00% |
| Wyoming | .00% | 1.00% |

numerous pools, the insurer will blend the interest rates and show the contractholder one effective rate.

## ■ GUARANTEE OF PRINCIPAL

Many fixed deferred annuities today guarantee the return of the contractholder's principal. This provision has been the backbone of the annuity contract from time in memoriam. Even some insurers that do not formally guarantee principal do return the contractholder's full premiums upon liquidation. Practitioners should, however, carefully read an annuity contract to determine if it does offer this guarantee.

From a marketing perspective, this guarantee of principal offers the practitioner the opportunity to position the fixed annuity as a retirement savings vehicle whose:

- underlying value will not fluctuate with interest rates and

- whose principal is not at risk.

This allows for favorable comparisons to bonds, bond funds and other interest sensitive investments that are subject to asset value fluctuation with interest rate changes. Safety of principal is a primary advantage of annuities and will be discussed in Chapter 8.

## ■ SUMMARY

In this chapter, we begin to see how annuities are constructed. Certainly, a key lesson to be learned is to read the annuity contract carefully to make sure that the features and benefits that you are representing are consistent with the actual contractual provisions of the policy. Understanding the contract and how it works is a critical part of the due care process that is every practitioner's responsibility to embrace.

## ■ CHAPTER 4 QUESTIONS FOR REVIEW

1. A guaranteed income stream cannot be created from a variable annuity.

   *True* or *False*

2. The new money method of crediting interest uses "buckets" or "pockets" to collect monies and credit interest rates.

   *True* or *False*

3. Portfolio renewal rates fluctuate much more significantly than new money rates.

   *True* or *False*

4. An indexed renewal interest rate will fluctuate according to the underlying index used by the insurer.

   *True* or *False*

5. The 10 percent free withdrawal privilege is usually noncumulative.

   *True* or *False*

6. All of the following are features of a single-premium deferred annuity, EXCEPT:

   a. There are usually no fees to buy the annuity.
   b. A higher rate may be credited for larger deposits.
   c. Monthly deposits of $25 are usually allowed.
   d. The minimum deposit to buy the annuity is usually $5,000.

7. Disintermediation is a risk that is accentuated when interest rates

   a. move up.
   b. move down.
   c. stay the same.
   d. interest rate movement does not affect the risk of disintermediation.

# Fixed Deferred Annuity Products

T he previous chapter was intended to serve as an introduction to fixed deferred annuities by focusing on the features and provisions that are common to all such products. Now we are ready to evaluate popular product designs offered for the fixed deferred annuity.

■■■■■

## ■ TRADITIONAL DEFERRED ANNUITY

In the early years of the deferred annuity, product designs were simple and straight-forward. Almost all products had an initial interest rate guarantee period (usually one year), an underlying minimum rate for the life of the contract (usually 4 percent) and surrender charges. Furthermore, most contracts allowed for some portion (usually 10 percent) of the annuity account to be withdrawn each year without charge. With traditional products, surrender charges sometimes lasted for a finite number of years (10 or so), although sometimes there was no limit to their duration. This basic annuity design has come to be known as the traditional, or "trust me," annuity. (See Ill. 5.1.)

### Product Design

The "trust me" moniker is not flattering. Because the initial rate was guaranteed only for a short period of time, the contractholder was at the mercy of the insurance company at the first and subsequent renewals. In effect, the contractholder had to trust the company to credit a fair and competitive renewal rate. If a reasonable rate was not established, the contractholder had little recourse because of the substantial surrender charge he or she would face upon liquidation. Many companies earned no one's trust as they sought to exploit this set of circumstances to enhance product profitability. This fact alone led to many of the new product designs explained next.

## ILL. 5.1 ■ *Typical Traditional or "Trust Me" Annuity*

| Year | Guaranteed Minimum Interest Rate | Typical Renewal Interest Rate* | Surrender Charge |
|------|------|------|------|
| 1 | 8.0% | — | 8% |
| 2 | 4.0% | 8.0% | 7% |
| 3 | 4.0% | 7.5% | 6% |
| 4 | 4.0% | 7.5% | 5% |
| 5 | 4.0% | 7.5% | 4% |
| 6 | 4.0% | 7.5% | 3% |
| 7 | 4.0% | 7.5% | 2% |
| 8 | 4.0% | 7.5% | 1% |
| 9+ | 4.0% | 7.5% | 0% |

*In a stable interest rate environment.

Traditional annuity products still exist today and look much the same as they did 10 years ago. The average duration of surrender charges is about 8 years, with most products ranging from 5 to 10 years.

## ■ INTEREST-INDEXED ANNUITY

One of the early product designs that was intended to provide an alternative to the traditional "trust me" concept was the *interest-indexed annuity*. There are currently two types of interest-indexed annuities available. One type provides complete protection in all types of interest rate environments and the other provides partial protection.

In either case, the annuity purchaser is given an initial interest rate guarantee (usually one year or less), and each renewal rate is tied to a published index, such as 10-year Treasury notes. This indexing provides consumer protection against arbitrary profit-enhancing renewal rates. Usually the indexing of renewals lasts only for the duration of the surrender charge period as the contractholder is then free to leave without penalty if he or she is unhappy with the renewal rate.

### Product Design

The interest-indexed products that provide complete protection typically have no restrictions on how far or how fast the renewal rates will move in relation to the index movement. (See Ill. 5.2.) From the insurer's perspective, this product requires some

### ILL. 5.2 ■ Interest-Indexed Annuity (Complete)

Minimum renewal indexed to 10-year Treasury note less 3.0 percent, 8.0 percent initial rate, 4.0 percent guaranteed minimum rate.

(Index in effect only during the eight-year surrender charge period.)

| Year | 10-Year Treasury Note | Minimum Renewal Rate | Minimum Rate if Nonindexed | Surrender Charge |
|---|---|---|---|---|
| 1 | 9.0% | — | 4.0% | 8% |
| 2 | 9.0% | 6.0 | 4.0% | 7% |
| 3 | 11.0% | 8.0 | 4.0% | 6% |
| 4 | 13.0% | 10.0 | 4.0% | 5% |
| 5 | 15.0% | 12.0 | 4.0% | 4% |
| 6 | 12.0% | 9.0 | 4.0% | 3% |
| 7 | 9.0% | 6.0 | 4.0% | 2% |
| 8 | 6.0% | 4.0 | 4.0% | 1% |
| 9+ | Not Relevant | 4.0 | 4.0% | 0% |

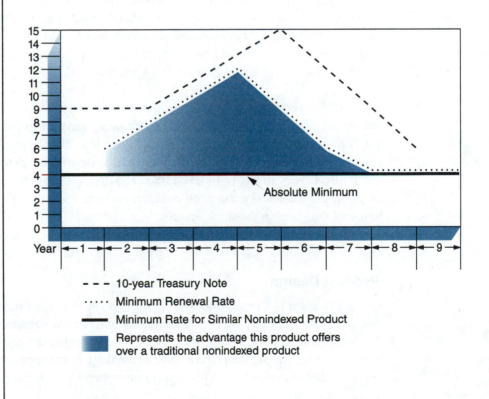

- – – 10-year Treasury Note
- ····· Minimum Renewal Rate
- —— Minimum Rate for Similar Nonindexed Product
- Represents the advantage this product offers over a traditional nonindexed product

fairly elaborate investment hedging techniques to protect against the effects of dramatic interest rate increases. These hedging techniques do carry a cost that is usually reflected in a lower first-year interest rate.

This type of product has become increasingly popular in recent years. However, keep in mind that two conditions must be satisfied for this product to be appealing. First, interest rates must be relatively low from a historical perspective *and* there must be a perception that rates will rise.

The partially indexed product normally has an overall cap on the rate the insurer guarantees at renewal. The insurer's purpose for imposing this cap is to alleviate the necessity of elaborate and expensive hedging techniques. Therefore, the partially indexed annuity primarily protects against the insurer lowering the renewal rate in a stable or increasing interest rate environment. It also insures that in a decreasing interest rate environment, the insurer can only lower renewal rates in a pattern consistent with the underlying index. (See Ill. 5.3.) These products have fallen out of favor recently; only a few are available today.

## ■ EQUITY-INDEXED ANNUITY PRODUCTS

Recent years have seen the advent of annuity products whose renewal interest rates are linked to some sort of stock market-related (equity) index, such as the Standard & Poor's 500 Index. These *equity-indexed annuity products* have experienced phenomenal growth in the past few years, primarily because of a low interest rate environment coupled with an explosive stock market.

Historically, people look for returns on their investments that outpace inflation and show real growth. In periods of low interest rates, real returns (returns after accounting for the effects of inflation) are usually quite low, and the stock market becomes the investment vehicle of choice. This attitude obviously favors the variable annuity, but it also favors an equity-indexed fixed annuity, whereby the client enjoys safety of principal and some guaranteed minimum returns (usually 3 percent) as well as some of the gains in the stock market.

### Product Design

Generally speaking, equity-indexed annuities do not have an initial interest rate guarantee period. Normally the contractholder is obligated to remain in the contract for some minimum period of time (five years or so) to enjoy the equity index return. A typical product would then return some percentage of the appreciation in the chosen equity index over that time. This percentage appreciation is called the *participation rate*.

The real challenge with equity-indexed products is understanding how they work. Today there are products that use average returns, point-to-point returns and high-

## ILL. 5.3 ■ Interest-Indexed Annuity (Partial)

**M**inimum renewal indexed to 10-year Treasury note less 2.0 percent, 8.0 percent initial rate, 4.0 percent guaranteed minimum rate.

(Index in effect only during the eight-year surrender charge period.)

| Year | 10-Year Treasury Note | Minimum Renewal Rate | Minimum Rate If Nonindexed | Surrender Charge |
|------|------------------------|----------------------|-----------------------------|------------------|
| 1 | 9.0% | — | 4.0% | 8% |
| 2 | 9.0% | 7.0 | 4.0% | 7% |
| 3 | 11.0% | 8.0 | 4.0% | 6% |
| 4 | 13.0% | 8.0 | 4.0% | 5% |
| 5 | 15.0% | 8.0 | 4.0% | 4% |
| 6 | 12.0% | 8.0 | 4.0% | 3% |
| 7 | 9.0% | 7.0 | 4.0% | 2% |
| 8 | 6.0% | 4.0 | 4.0% | 1% |
| 9+ | Not Relevant | 4.0 | 4.0% | 0% |

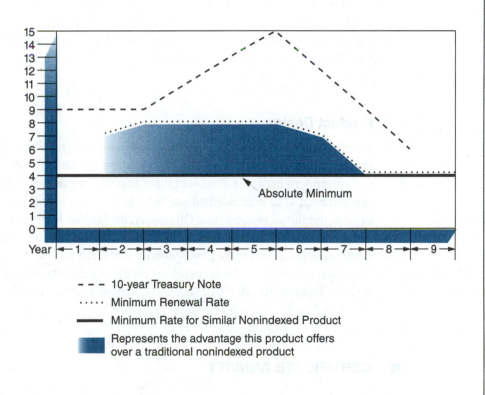

- - - 10-year Treasury Note

· · · · · Minimum Renewal Rate

——— Minimum Rate for Similar Nonindexed Product

Represents the advantage this product offers over a traditional nonindexed product

water-mark returns. There are also products that combine two or three of these methodologies in one product. More than 20 products are on the market today and no two work the same way. This makes it very difficult to compare products and potential returns. An extra degree of diligence is required to become educated about these products as is a commitment to educate consumers so they buy products best suited to their needs.

From the insurer's prospective, equity-indexed products are very difficult to invest. Typically, elaborate hedging instruments must be purchased against the chosen index. The costs of such hedges must be closely managed to provide for the necessity of principal guarantee and minimum return safety for the contractholder. The advent of new, sophisticated financial products has made this possible within the last few years.

## ■ BAILOUT ANNUITY

The *bailout annuity* was yet another product design to provide an alternative to the "trust me" concept. The added protection the bailout provides is similar in nature to that of the partial interest index. Basically, it protects against the insurer lowering renewal rates in a steady or rising interest rate environment. There are those who argue the bailout goes one step further and provides protection against the lowering of renewal rates when interest rates are falling. That argument is weak—though not entirely invalid—because the consumer, in a falling interest rate environment, will only have the option to go to other products with equally low rates.

### Product Design

Here's how the bailout works. The basic product design is usually traditional except for the bailout feature, which allows the contractholder to liquidate the annuity without surrender charges in the event that the renewal rate falls below a predescribed interest rate. That predescribed rate is known as the *bailout rate* and is usually set at or near the initial interest rate. Obviously, the bailout feature is only relevant during the surrender charge period. Anytime thereafter the contractholder can liquidate the contract without surrender penalty under any circumstances. In recent years, reserving requirements have been increased on these products, making them more expensive for insurers to offer. Consequently, their popularity has diminished.

## ■ CERTIFICATE ANNUITY

As annuity providers became more sophisticated in their marketing efforts, they began to design products that more closely resembled those of the competition. Because an annuity is a safe place to invest money at a fixed return, the bank certificate of deposit became the target competition. These products have come to be known as *certificate* or *CD annuities*. We are not inclined to encourage the use of the name "CD" annuity, because it may imply that the product is backed or guaranteed by a bank or the Federal Department Insurance Corporation (FDIC). Therefore, we encourage the use of "certificate," because these products are sometimes offered as group contracts with the client as the certificateholder.

## Product Design

Certificate annuities come in many shapes and sizes. Because these products have met with outstanding success, some companies for marketing purposes are calling even their traditional products certificate annuities. Therefore, it has become important to understand and define exactly what is meant by "certificate annuity."

A certificate annuity is any product in which the initial interest rate guarantee period precisely parallels the surrender charge period. In other words, if the product's initial interest rate is 8 percent guaranteed for three years with three years of surrender charges, then it's a certificate annuity. If the product has a 30-day window of surrenderability following the three-year guarantee period for free surrenders, then begins a new surrender charge period with a new three-year guarantee, it too is a certificate annuity. This is because the contractholder is free to surrender, without charge, prior to locking in again to a new period. It is not a coincidence that this design is almost identical to a bank CD.

Certificate annuities may range from one to ten years in duration. It is important to note that these products present a unique investment challenge for the insurance company. The carrier must use some "bullet" investment techniques where the underlying investments are liquid at the exact time that contractholders arrive at their window of free surrenderability. Otherwise, insurers would experience significant investment losses in stable or rising interest rate environments.

## Nonsurrenderable Certificate Annuities

The last few years have also seen the advent of *nonsurrenderable certificate annuities*. A nonsurrenderable product shares all of the same attributes as the surrenderable annuity except liquidity. During the guarantee period, a surrenderable annuity can be entirely liquidated, subject to a surrender charge. The nonsurrenderable annuity cannot be liquidated until the end of the guarantee period, during the surrenderable window. Of course, most nonsurrenderable annuities carry some measure of liquidity, such as 10 percent free withdrawals or loan features, as discussed in Chapter 4.

## ■ MARKET VALUE ADJUSTED ANNUITY

Another product design that has surfaced in recent years is the *market value adjusted,* or *MVA, annuity.* The MVA annuity shifts some but not all of the investment risk from the insurer to the contractholder in the sense that the annuity account value will fluctuate as market interest rates fluctuate. Within limitations, the theory of MVAs is exactly that of asset value fluctuation in bonds. It is beyond the scope of this text to describe the theory of bond value fluctuation as a function of market interest rates, but it is well recognized that as interest rates move up, bond values will move down and as interest rates move down, bond values will move up. A simple way of understanding this would be to think of yourself as the owner of a 20-year bond purchased in 1981, paying 15 percent interest. The bond matures in 2001. Interest rates have come down quite a bit since 1981. A comparable bond might pay 8 percent interest today. Is your bond paying 15 percent worth more or less than one paying 8 percent? Of course it's worth more. That is why it can carry a higher price (asset value).

Market value adjusted annuities work similarly but can provide some protection. Unlike the bond in the above example, the MVA annuity will usually contain a floor limiting how low the asset value can go. The amount at risk with an MVA product is normally limited to amounts in excess of the premiums paid plus interest, accrued at the minimum guaranteed level in the contract. There will likely be continued growth in MVA annuities in the future, since they offer the insurer some protection against disintermediation while also providing some minimum guarantees to the contractholder.

MVA annuity buyers experience higher interest rates (all other things being equal) than traditional annuity buyers. This is because the insurer can pass on some risk to the buyer. Furthermore, MVAs have lower reserving requirements, a feature which also saves the insurer money. There has been some debate as to whether the higher rates enjoyed by the consumer offset the additional risk he or she assumes. There is no easy answer to this debate; however, it is fair to say that fixed annuity buyers buy primarily for safety. Certainly one element of the safety equation is removed with an MVA annuity. The practitioner must take care to disclose this market risk inherent to an MVA annuity when discussing these products with prospects or clients.

---

### ILL. 5.4 ■ *Registered MVA Products*

There are a number of MVA products on the market today that are similar to those described in the text, except they do not offer a guarantee of principal or minimum interest. In other words, the market value adjustment can be sufficiently negative to cause a loss of principal, even if the contractholder has owned the contract for a number of years. The market conditions that would bring this about would be a rapid and substantial rise in interest rates. Because of this risk, these kinds of MVA products must be registered as securities. Thus, they fall under the category of variable annuities (the subject of Chapter 6), even though they more closely resemble fixed annuities.

## ■ BONUS RATE ANNUITY

The fact that annuities carry surrender charges makes for some interesting possibilities that do not exist for other financial instruments. As noted previously, the traditional "trust me" annuity design has an interest rate guarantee period, such as one year, and it is always shorter than the surrender charge period. Consequently, various product design features (bailout, index, etc.) were developed to give some rate protection to the contractholder.

The past few years have also seen another interesting phenomenon develop. Companies are now including some type of *bonus rate* in the first year. For example, let's say that the prevailing annuity interest rate is 7 percent. A bonus rate product may offer 8 percent in year one and disclose it as 7 percent plus a 1 percent bonus. This bonus is really nothing more than an inducement to buy, usually because prevailing interest rates are low.

Two words of caution. First, someone has to "pay" for these bonus rates and it is usually *not* the insurer. It is either the consumer or the practitioner. The practitioner "pays" by taking a lower commission; the contractholder "pays" by subsequent year renewal rates that are lower than what he or she otherwise would have received. Second, insurers often offer first-year bonuses and don't reveal that fact. In other words, using the example above, the contractholder is led to believe that 8 percent is the prevailing rate. He or she only finds out otherwise when the first renewal rate drops by 1 percent or more. It's too late by that time because he or she is locked into the contract by high surrender charges. Quite often, the best performing product is not the product with the highest first-year rate.

## ■ TWO-TIERED ANNUITY

Among certain producer groups, primarily TSA producers, the *two-tiered annuity* has been extremely popular for many years. However, with the advent of more consumer-oriented products and a more skeptical look by the National Association of Insurance Commissioners (NAIC), the popularity of the two-tiered design has waned. As a matter of fact, the two-tiered annuity design has been banned by some states.

Here's how it works. Usually, the first-year interest rate is quite high relative to the market, as are subsequent guarantees. Commissions are also typically high relative to other products. The insurer is able to offer high rates and high commissions because those rates are predicated on the assumption the contractholder will stay with the product through annuitization. Sometimes term certain annuitization is allowed, but most often the annuitization option must be life contingent. If the contractholder does not stay through annuitization but instead elects to surrender prior to that time, he or she will be assessed an applicable surrender charge and be retroactively credited with lower interest rates back to the inception of the contract. In

---

### ILL. 5.5 ■ *Typical Deferred Annuity Product Characteristics*

- Initial interest rate guarantee period, such as one, three or five years

- Five- to ten-year surrender charge period

- Guarantee of principal

- 4 percent minimum lifetime interest rate

---

other words, the contractholder gets one tier of interest rates by staying with the contract through annuitization and another, lower tier of rates if he or she does not.

Potential purchasers of a two-tiered annuity—and those who sell these products—must be certain that they can trust the insurer to offer strength, stability and competitive returns throughout the period of deferral and annuitization (which may mean a lifetime). Otherwise, the choice to surrender the contract early can be extremely expensive.

## ■ SUMMARY

It is impossible to evaluate and discuss all possible fixed deferred annuity products in the scope of one chapter. However, the product designs and features presented here represent those that are the most widely offered and readily available today. It's important to recognize that all deferred annuity products will share some characteristics of those we've described. Typical characteristics can be found in Ill. 5.5.

## ■ CHAPTER 5 QUESTIONS FOR REVIEW

1. Nonsurrenderable certificate annuities usually have a window of surrenderability at the end of the guarantee period.

   *True* or *False*

2. A typical minimum interest rate for a deferred annuity is 2 percent.

   *True* or *False*

3. A standard free withdrawal provision specifies

   a. free withdrawals are allowed after 10 years.
   b. 10 percent annual free withdrawals are allowed.
   c. 10 percent of any withdrawal is subject to surrender charges.
   d. 10 percent of any withdrawal is free of surrender charges.

4. The "trust me" name for traditional annuities comes from the fact that

   a. everyone trusts insurance companies.
   b. no one trusts insurance companies.
   c. one needs to trust that the insurer will credit a fair renewal rate.
   d. no one trusts insurance practitioners to sell the appropriate annuity.

5. In a rising interest rate environment, all of the following are true EXCEPT:

   a. A complete index annuity renewal rate will rise.
   b. The account value of a market value adjusted annuity will fall.
   c. A partial index annuity renewal rate may not rise but will not fall.
   d. Renewal rates on traditional products will rise because of the minimum guarantee protection.

6. To which of the following would an equity-indexed annuity link its renewal rate?

   a. 10-year Treasury notes
   b. Standard & Poor's 500 Index
   c. Current money market rates
   d. Cost-of-living adjustments as determined by the IRS

# 6

# Variable Annuities

I n previous chapters, we discussed general features of fixed annuity products and different types of fixed deferred and immediate annuities. We now move into the arena of variable returns, potential risk of principal and the opportunity to grab the "brass investment ring." Let's begin to learn about variable annuities.

■ ■ ■ ■ ■

## ■ WHAT IS A VARIABLE ANNUITY?

A *variable annuity* is just as its name implies: an annuity whose return is not certain, like the fixed annuity, but variable. The components of a variable annuity are split into a *general account* and a *separate account*. Contractholders can choose how to allocate their premium deposits among various options within the two accounts, depending on their risk tolerance and how they believe the stock, bond and money markets are going to perform. A certain percentage of each premium can be directed into the separate account, which houses the variable investment options; the balance is placed in the general account, which performs like a traditional annuity. In some cases, a contractholder may wish to be 100 percent invested in either the general or separate account. Illustration 6.1 shows how premium dollars may be split into the separate and general accounts.

On further review we see that the variable annuity is a hybrid of a fixed annuity and a mutual fund. However, unlike a mutual fund, the variable annuity is tax deferred and also has a death benefit to provide protection should the annuitant die during a period when the contract's account value is less than the amount of premiums deposited into the annuity.

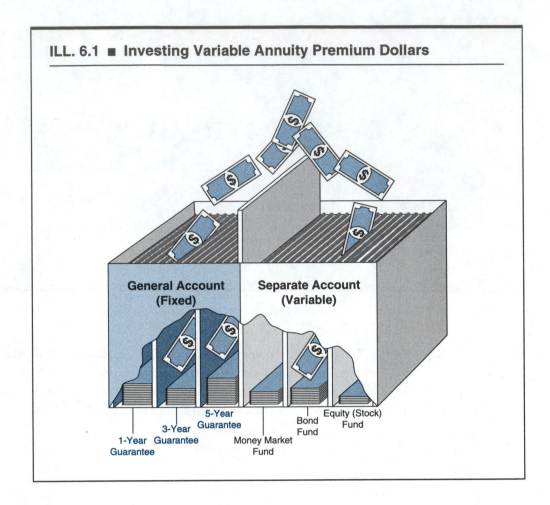

ILL. 6.1 ■ Investing Variable Annuity Premium Dollars

## ■ HISTORY OF VARIABLE ANNUITIES

Though life insurance companies have been offering variable annuities since the mid-1950s, the greatest growth in the market has taken place over the past five years. Variable annuity sales in 1990 were $18 billion as compared to only $2.5 billion in 1980. That growth trend continued through the mid-1990s, with variable annuity sales exceeding $50 billion in 1995. Another trend becoming evident is the mix between sales of fixed annuities and variable annuities and the mix between allocations to the fixed and separate accounts. Historically, the fixed annuity has outsold the variable annuity, three or four to one in any given year. In recent years, however, this mix has been approximately 50/50. In addition, approximately 40 percent of the premiums going into variable annuities have traditionally been directed into the general account which generates fixed returns and is not subject to market fluctuations, but recently, there has been a reduction in the percentage of variable annuity premiums dollars that are being deposited into the general account.

During the past decade, the variable annuity has seen a number of changes, including tax law changes that have affected both it and the fixed annuity. As more and more potential investors learn about the benefits of variable annuities, the division between the dollars invested in fixed and variable annuities will continue to narrow.

## Variable Annuities and Uncle Sam

Back in the mid- to late 1970s, a variable annuity could be "wrapped" around almost any investment, thereby creating a tax-deferred product. For example, one could buy IBM stock and wrap that stock in a variable annuity. At the death of the annuitant, the beneficiary received a stepped-up cost basis on the annuity, meaning that the beneficiary paid no income taxes on the growth. Investors would wrap stocks, bonds and real estate in the old variable annuity to get the advantage of the stepped-up cost basis. For rather obvious reasons, Congress took away the stepped-up basis on annuities in 1977 and eliminated the wraparound annuity altogether.

As the decade of the 1980s began, variable annuities found new life. A number of new products were introduced, spearheaded once again by the newly found stock-brokerage distribution system. The new variable annuity products simply used popular existing mutual funds and wrapped them in a variable annuity shell.

As an example, Massachusetts Financial Services took its very popular family of mutual funds and wrapped them in a variable annuity called Spectrum—same managers, same funds, but with the benefit of tax deferral. Again, Congress saw this as abusive, stepped in and created the rules that we live with today in the variable annuity market. In essence, Congress said that a variable annuity had to have its own separate funds, which cannot be commingled with other mutual fund assets. This required the creation of separate funds and separate prospectuses, specifically for the variable annuity.

These new funds obviously had no prior performance, even though they might have been managed by the same portfolio manager that managed the mutual funds. Because there was no performance history, it took years for the distributors of these new products to become comfortable enough in the underlying fund performance to effectively market the new variable annuities. In addition, the industry struggled with the cumulative effect of all the tax law changes. Distributors became paralyzed by the thought of future tax law changes and the effect they may have on annuity products in general and variable products specifically.

By the mid-1980s, however, the variable annuity showed signs of life as the major wire houses began to focus heavily on the product as an alternative to fixed annuities. Variable annuity sales grew, with a small downturn in the late '80s as a result of market conditions. In the early 1990s, variable annuities really caught fire, with new product enhancements like death benefit resets (discussed later in this chapter). Sales were further helped by a low interest rate environment.

## The Variable Annuity Today

The growth in variable annuities has been nothing less than explosive. With variable annuity sales in excess of $50 billion a year, the industry continues to expand as alternative distributors such as banks begin to focus their marketing attention on these products. But what forces have been driving this craze?

During the mid-1990s, interest rates on fixed annuities fell to historic lows. Just as interest rates were bottoming, the stock market took off, with the Dow Jones gaining over 33 percent in 1995. The combination of these two events brought a significant influx of new money into the variable annuity product line. Money came from owners of CDs and money market funds as well as from fixed annuity owners whose renewal rates were falling as interest rates declined.

Another reason for the growth of variable annuities has been the aging of the baby boomer. This huge market segment, now beginning to enter their 50s, is more risk tolerant than their mothers and fathers who bought fixed annuities 10 to 15 years ago. Using variable annuities, these baby boomers are investing heavily in the market, using some of the advanced product features we'll be discussing in this chapter.

As a result of this recent growth, more and more mutual fund companies are looking to partner with insurance companies to offer proprietary variable annuities. These partnerships have prompted no-load mutual fund companies such as Fidelity, Vanguard, T. Rowe Price and Dreyfus to create their own products to compete with load companies that have long had their own product platform, including Franklin Funds, American Funds and AIM Weingarten. Though not a mutual fund company, Charles Schwab has also created its own annuity for Schwab customers and a number of banks have created their own proprietary annuities using their mutual funds.

## ■ FEATURES OF THE VARIABLE ANNUITY

Just as there are characteristics of the fixed deferred annuity that are consistent from product to product, so too are there certain features shared by all variable annuities. For purposes of our discussion, we will start with the basic chassis used in the variable annuity and then add on the optional benefits that are currently being designed into new versions of the variable products.

### Separate Account

As previously noted, the variable annuity is characterized by a *separate account* that houses all of the variable account options. The separate account is so called because it is not part of the general account assets of the insurance company. These are the investment fund options or subaccounts that comprise the variable annuity.

Actually, the separate account is maintained solely for the purpose of making investments for the contractholder. This transfers the risk from the insurer to the contractholder. The separate accounts are *not* insured by the carrier, except in the event of the owner's or annuitant's death. What happens to the separate account in those circumstances will be discussed later in this chapter. Account values will fluctuate, depending specifically on the performance of the underlying investments. All profits and losses, minus fees, are passed along to the contractholder. In the highly unlikely event the insurance company becomes insolvent, separate accounts are not attachable by the insurer's creditors and are normally distributed immediately to the contractholders. A wide variety of funds is available to the contractholder in the separate account. These alternatives will be discussed in detail later in this chapter.

### General Account

The *general account* of an insurance company houses all of its assets. Within the general account, the insurance company will offer the fixed account option or options that complement the variable annuity separate account choices. The fixed account can be structured in any number of ways, but it most frequently looks like a traditional fixed annuity, many with multiple-year interest rate guarantees. Many variable annuities offer fixed accounts with interest rate guarantees from one to ten years.

In addition to a guaranteed rate of interest, the fixed account offers a guarantee of principal. In this respect, it differs from the separate account. However, to provide the type of flexibility that is crucial to the variable annuity, the contractholder is given the right to transfer from the general account to the separate account and vice versa. Transfers from the general account to the separate account, though allowed,

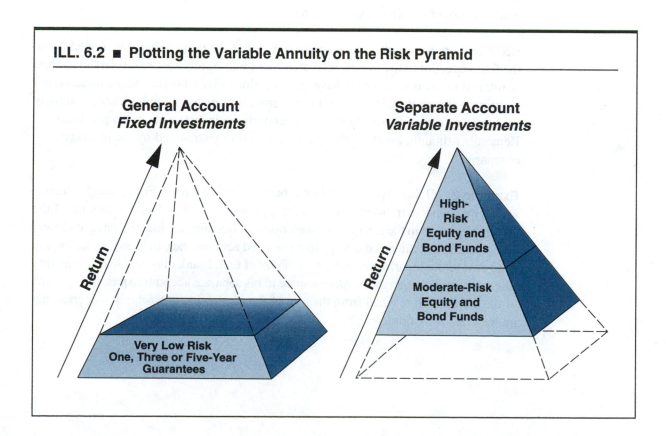

### ILL. 6.2 ■ Plotting the Variable Annuity on the Risk Pyramid

**General Account**
*Fixed Investments*

Return

Very Low Risk
One, Three or Five-Year
Guarantees

**Separate Account**
*Variable Investments*

Return

High-
Risk
Equity and
Bond Funds

Moderate-Risk
Equity and
Bond Funds

may require a *market value adjustment* (MVA) and will likely be limited to a certain percentage of the amount in the fixed account.

The concept of market value adjustments was first discussed in Chapter 5. With reference to variable annuities, they are needed to provide the insurance company with some protection, should a contractholder wish to transfer funds prior to the end of the surrender charge period or the end of the specific interest rate guarantee period within the fixed account. Depending on where current interest rates are relative to when premiums were invested in the general account, the contractholder may or may not have an additional cost when moving money to the separate account or surrendering the policy. Let's look at a couple of examples.

**Example 1.**   Frank owns a variable annuity that has three separate account investment options and a general account option offering one fixed interest rate. The separate account options are a money market fund, a bond fund and a stock fund. The fixed option is a one-year guarantee, with one-year renewal rates. The surrender charges on the contract are 5 percent of the account value for six years, and there is a market value adjustment during these six years.

Frank directs the insurer to allocate 60 percent of his funds to the separate account and 40 percent to the one-year guaranteed fixed account. The fixed account rate is 8 percent. Three years later, current interest rates have gone from 8 percent to 10 percent. Frank wants to move from the 8 percent fixed account to the separate money market account within the variable annuity.

Because there is a market value adjustment, all of the money that was moved from the fixed account to the money market account will be adjusted based on the change in interest rates. Because rates have gone up since Frank purchased the annuity, an additional charge is levied against his account to compensate the insurance company for losses as it may be forced to sell the underlying investments in the portfolio. Remember though, Frank's principal is most likely guaranteed by the insurance company.

**Example 2.**   If, however, interest rates have gone down since Frank bought the policy, he may wish to transfer funds into the separate account and take advantage of the potential growth in the separate account options. Because the interest rates are lower than when Frank allocated money into the fixed account, he can transfer that money at no cost to the separate account. As a matter of fact, Frank may find that his insurer, like many, will even transfer more money to his separate account to pass along some of the gain which resulted from the sale of the underlying portfolio in a decreasing interest rate environment.

## The Prospectus

As noted in Chapter 1, variable annuities are considered securities and must be registered with the SEC. The SEC requires that all variable annuity sales materials include a prospectus, which contains all of the relevant information regarding the contract. While not a terribly appealing marketing document, the prospectus is a valuable tool for the practitioner. A thorough review of this document will reveal any hidden charges not clearly defined in the supporting marketing materials. The prospectus outlines all costs and benefits, defines terms, discusses the issuer and likely gives the potential contractholder more information than he or she wants to digest at any one time. However, used properly, the prospectus can be an effective sales tool.

As valuable as a prospectus is, most consumers find these documents difficult to understand. In an effort to ease the confusion caused by both the length and wording of the prospectus, the SEC now allows an insurer to provide a "Profile" along with the regular statutory prospectus. The Profile, approved on a trial basis in 1996, is an extract of the important information contained in a prospectus, designed to summarize and explain essential points in a way that is understandable by the average investor. It will also enable consumers to more easily compare variable annuity products. The overwhelming sentiment is that as a result of the Profile, consumers will be better informed and more knowledgeable about the products they're purchasing.

To create and use a Profile, companies must conform to a set of guidelines created by the National Association for Variable Annuities (NAVA) which was instrumental in the development of the Profile. The Guidelines for the Variable Annuity Profile describe certain disclosure items that must be included in the Profile, including information about the annuity contract, annuity payments, purchases, investment options, expenses, withdrawals, performance and death benefits. The order in which these items must appear is specified in the Guidelines and the content of the Profile is limited to that set forth in the Guidelines. The NAVA Guidelines are reproduced in Ill. 6.3.

## Annuity Accumulation Units

The variable annuity differs significantly from the fixed annuity in that investment dollars are converted into *accumulation units* that are based on the net asset value of the underlying mutual fund at the time of purchase. The insurer converts the premium deposit made by the contractholder into units based on this net asset value, as described in Ill. 6.4. The only exception to this is the money market account whose net asset value is maintained on a constant dollar basis, where one dollar buys one unit. As a result, the money market account credits a stated interest rate that changes as the underlying assets of the money market change.

# Guidelines for the Variable Annuity Profile

### March 19, 1996

*Purpose. The purpose of the Profile is to provide consumers with a consistent and readable document that allows easy comparability with other Variable Annuity Profiles.*

*General.* A Profile will be considered part of the prospectus which constitutes Part A of a registration statement on Form N-4 under the securities laws. It should be used in one of the following formats: (i) as a prospectus wrapper, or (ii) as a separate document that would accompany the full prospectus. The full prospectus may omit the information required by Item 3(b) ("Synopsis of Information") if a Profile is used. The information required by Items 3(a) and 4(a) of Form N-4 must be included in the full prospectus where required by Form N-4.

The name of the life insurance company and type or name of annuity contract (e.g., "Variable and Fixed Annuity Contract" or "Immediate Variable Annuity Contract" or "ABC Variable Annuity") must appear prominently at the beginning of the document. The document should be prominently identified as a "Profile" (either alone or in conjunction with the name or type of contract, e.g., "Variable Annuity Contract Profile") at the beginning of the document to inform the reader as to the nature of the document. Reference to a "Profile Prospectus" should not be made. The Profile must be dated. The following legend must appear prominently in the Profile:

**This Profile is a summary of some of the more important points that you should know and consider before purchasing the Contract. The Contract is more fully described [later in this Prospectus][in the full Prospectus which accompanies this Profile]. Please read the prospectus carefully.**

A Profile must include the eleven disclosure items in the order listed. In the interest of standardization, all items must be numbered. Include the appropriate heading, although a heading may be presented in the form of a question (e.g., "How to Purchase?").

The contents of the Profile must be limited to the information set forth in these Guidelines. Additional information, or more detailed responses to the items listed, may only be disclosed in a separate document (except for any legends that may be required by law). Except as discussed below and the legend above, the Profile should not contain cross-references to the full prospectus or to any other document. The use of footnotes should be avoided, if possible.

The purpose of the Profile is to provide a summary of the essential information about the variable annuity contract in a way that is understandable by the average investor. THE PROFILE MUST BE CLEAR, CONCISE AND UNDERSTANDABLE.

THE USE OF TECHNICAL OR LEGAL TERMS, COMPLEX LANGUAGE, OR EXCESSIVE DETAIL SHOULD BE AVOIDED.

*Disclosure Items.*

The disclosure items are as follows:

1. **The Annuity Contract**.

    Briefly describe the variable annuity contract(s) offered by the prospectus, including the investment risks borne by the investor. Describe the accumulation phase and the annuity phase. State that the amount of money accumulated during the accumulation phase will determine the amount of annuity payments during the annuity phase. If a general account option is offered, the registrant can so indicate.

2. **Annuity Payments**.

    State on what basis the Contract can be annuitized, i.e., fixed only, variable only, or fixed and variable. Briefly describe the annuity options.

3. **Purchase**.

    Briefly describe how to purchase the Contract. Describe any minimum purchase payments. Describe who can purchase the contract.

4. **Investment Options**.

    State the name of each portfolio or series available as an investment option under the

*Source:* Reprinted with permission from the National Association for Variable Annuities.

contract. A detailed explanation of the structure of the separate account, sub-accounts and underlying funds is not necessary and should be avoided.

5. **Expenses**.

This section has two components. First, it should set out, as a narrative, all of the charges assessed under the Contract including the charges assessed at the underlying fund level. Registrants may, but are not required to, list separately the components of their insurance charge (e.g., if the separate account asset charges are 1.4%, the registrant may state that 1.25% is for mortality and expense risk and .15% is for administration). Registrants may use a table to describe any contingent deferred sales charge if the use of such a table makes the information more understandable to the investor. The second component is a chart which sets forth by portfolio or series the charges under the contract. The first column should show the total annual insurance charges (including any contract maintenance charge converted to a percentage). The second column should show the total annual portfolio charges. The third column should be the total annual charges under the contract and is calculated by aggregating the charges set forth in the first two columns. The fourth and fifth columns contained in the chart are examples which show the expenses, including any contingent deferred sales charges, incurred under the contract of 1 year and for 10 years. The instruction contained in Form N-4, Item 3(a) with respect to the

calculation of the examples are to be referred to in determining how to calculate the examples contained in the Profile. This item should contain a cross-reference to the complete fee table contained in the prospectus. If there were expense reimbursements or fee waiver arrangements that reduced any operating expenses, the fact that such reimbursements or waivers exist should be disclosed. Do not show the amount the expenses would have been absent the reimbursement or waiver. Footnotes should not be used in preparing the chart required by this Item.

6. **Taxes**.

Briefly describe the tax laws applicable to the Contract.

7. **Access To Your Money**.

Briefly describe the conditions under which an owner can withdraw some or all of the value of his or her contract. Include a brief description of any deferred sales charge, including any waivers, and a statement that the withdrawal may be subject to income tax and to a penalty.

8. **Performance**.

Present in tabular format the total return, set forth as a percentage, for each investment option for each of the last 10 calendar years (or less if inception date is less than ten years previous). Performance figures should be shown for complete years only (no stub period performance). In determining total return include the effect of all recurring expenses such as any contract maintenance fee. Do not include front end or deferred sales charges in the total return calculation. The

total amount of the charges included in this Item should equal the total annual charges set forth in the third column of the chart required by Item 5. Include a statement identifying the expenses that have been included in determining the total return percentages and that past performance does not guarantee future results. If applicable, disclose that the performance figures do not reflect front end or deferred sales charges imposed under the contract and that if such charges were reflected, they would have the effect of reducing performance. No other performance figures may be shown in response to this item.

9. **Death Benefits**.

Briefly describe the death benefit under the Contract.

10. **Other Information**.

Registrants should briefly describe any other information they deem relevant to purchasers. The following are examples of such items: any free look provisions, whether the contract is a group or individual contract, any additional contract features (e.g., dollar cost averaging, systematic withdrawals, and nursing home or terminal illness riders). Registrants should take caution in drafting this section in that it should not add unnecessarily to the length of the Profile. Confusing names should not be used without explanation.

11. **Inquiries**.

State the address and telephone numbers where interested persons can call or write to obtain more information.

*Source:* Reprinted with permission from the National Association for Variable Annuities.

### ILL. 6.4 ■ *Calculating Accumulation Unit Value*

| | |
|---|---:|
| Total value of all fund securities: | $2,372,496 |
| Less prorated management fees: | − 118,625 |
| Less prorated expenses: | − 62,918 |
| | $2,190,953 |
| Divided by number of outstanding shares: | ÷ 13,296 |
| Equals accumulation unit value: | $ 164.78 |

Illustration 6.4 shows how the annuity accumulation units are determined and valued. The total value of all assets within the mutual fund, less a prorated share of management fees and expenses, is divided by the number of outstanding shares. The annuity accumulation unit value (AUV) is calculated on a daily basis.

## Variable Annuity Costs

Variable annuities are also distinct from fixed annuities in that there are different costs associated with them. Aside from the surrender charges which are similar to the fixed annuity, variable annuity costs are driven more by the increased asset management and administration costs that are inherent in the product.

### Contract Maintenance Charge

Each insurance company will assess a yearly *maintenance charge* to cover the administrative expenses associated with the variable annuity contract. This charge, usually assessed at each contract anniversary date and upon surrender of the contract, covers the cost of issuing the policy, as well as other administrative costs. In our sample policy in Ill. 6.5, the yearly maintenance charge is $30.

### Administrative Service Charge

An *administrative service charge* is usually expressed as a percentage of the funds invested in the separate accounts. It covers the cost of transferring funds from one separate account option to other separate account options or to the general account fixed option. It also covers the issuance of quarterly, semiannual or annual statements, depending on the insurer. Finally, it covers the costs of tracking deposits and the issuance of confirmations when monies are received or withdrawals are made. (This would include the processing of loans for variable annuities that are used to fund qualified plans such as 403(b), 401(k) or 401(a) plans.) This fee is calculated and deducted daily on an annualized basis from all monies in the separate/variable

**ILL. 6.5 ■ *Typical Variable Annuity Contract Charges***

**ABC Variable Annuity**

| | |
|---|---|
| Contract Maintenance Charge | $30 |
| Administrative Service Charge | .15% |
| Mortality and Expense Risk Charge | 1.25% |
| Contingent Deferred Sales Charge: | |
| Year 1 | 7.00% |
| 2 | 6.00% |
| 3 | 5.00% |
| 4 | 4.00% |
| 5 | 3.00% |
| 6 | 2.00% |
| 7 | 1.00% |

accounts within the contract. In our sample policy shown in Ill. 6.5, the administrative service charge is .15 percent (15 basis points), or $1.50 for every $1,000 of invested separate account funds.

### Mortality and Expense Risk Charge

One of the key components of the variable annuity is the death benefit. The death benefit provision can be structured in a number of different ways and will be discussed later in this chapter. For purposes of understanding its cost, most insurance companies split the cost of the mortality risk and expense, with mortality risk running at 70 to 80 basis points of invested assets, or $7 to $8 per $1,000. The mortality risk is usually defined as the risk of the annuitant dying while the account balance is below the cumulative total of premiums paid, less withdrawals. This would require the insurance company to pay the beneficiary a benefit partly from the insurer's earnings or reserves.

The expense portion of the charge provides the margin of safety the company needs to guarantee that administrative costs will not exceed the .15 percent stated in the contract, which translates into $1.50 per $1,000. The total of the mortality risk and expense risk charges should be anywhere from .50 to 1.55 percent per year. Most insurers calculate and deduct this expense daily on an annualized basis. The sample policy in Ill. 6.5 charges a combined 1.25 percent mortality and expense risk charge.

Some of the newer approaches to defining and periodically resetting the death benefit under a variable annuity contract (discussed later in this chapter) are more expensive for the insurer. Consequently, some carriers assess an additional mortality charge above and beyond those discussed here. The extra charge ranges from 8 to 15 basis points. Some carriers allow the buyer to choose between the traditional death benefit reset and the enhanced benefit reset at the higher cost.

Keep in mind that the mortality risk and expense risk charges, as well as the administrative service charges, are only assessed against the funds held in the separate account; they are never assessed against funds held in the general account.

### Contingent Deferred Sales Charge

Most variable annuities are currently marketed without a front-end load. This means that 100 percent of the contractholder's funds are available for immediate investment through the fixed and separate account options. In return, to offset commissions that the insurance company pays to the practitioner who sold the contract, the company will apply surrender charges to contractholders who liquidate their contracts during the first several years. These surrender charges may also be called *contingent deferred sales charges*. In the Ill. 6.5 sample policy, the contingent deferred sales charge is 7 percent of withdrawals that exceed 10 percent of the premiums paid into the contract, reducing by 1 percent each year. The charge is assessed against any withdrawal that does not meet the free withdrawal provision of the contract. These free withdrawal privileges, introduced in Chapter 4, will be discussed in detail shortly.

### Separate Account Expenses

The final charges that we will discuss are the expenses associated specifically with the separate account investment options. These charges are levied by the fund managers and break down into two types: *management fees* and *fund expenses*.

Management fees are simply the cost of managing the portfolio in the separate account. Historically, these fees were paid to the insurer's in-house asset manager. Today, however, they are more likely to be what the insurance company must pay to an outside fund manager or managers, as many insurers have now contracted the fund management to a mutual fund company. Management fees range widely, depending on the type of fund. The range is generally from .25 percent of assets under management for a money market fund to around 1 percent for some of the global or international funds. The difference reflects the level of expertise needed to manage the fund and the higher costs associated with the start-up of any fund. Money market funds, for example, tend to be less complicated to manage than some of the newer, more exotic international funds, which require considerable research on the part of the fund manager.

In addition to portfolio management fees, there are also expenses associated with running these funds. These mutual fund expenses include the cost of buying and selling securities as well as administering the trades. Fees range from 5 basis points for money market funds up to 75 to 100 basis points on the more expensive global funds.

## ILL. 6.6 ■ Separate Account Expenses

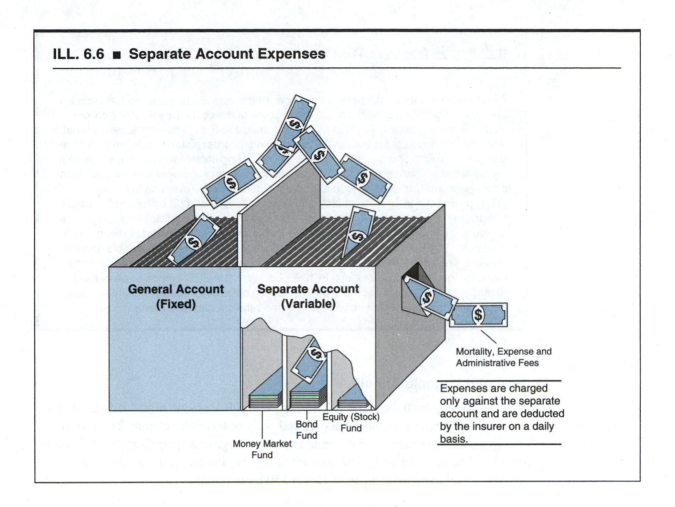

General Account (Fixed)

Separate Account (Variable)

Money Market Fund

Bond Fund

Equity (Stock) Fund

Mortality, Expense and Administrative Fees

Expenses are charged only against the separate account and are deducted by the insurer on a daily basis.

It is important to understand that both management fees and expense charges are *not* assessed directly to the contractholder. They will *not* show up on the contractholder's statements. These charges are assessed against the subaccount values and are subtracted before calculating the accumulation unit value for the subaccount, just as they are in mutual funds.

One final point regarding fund management charges should be noted. While these fund management charges are not assessed directly to the contractholder, they are charged against the fund itself. As such, the charges will affect the performance of the underlying fund. Some managers will attempt to build a particular subaccount—for example, a global subaccount—by subsidizing the expense charges in the account. This subsidization will extend only for a limited period of time. After that, full charges will be deducted. If the account is still small, those charges could be considerable and might have a significant effect on performance.

To determine whether a fund manager is subsidizing the subaccount, take a look at the prospectus. The prospectus will detail the level of subsidization and the length of time that the subsidization will be in effect.

> ### ILL. 6.7 ■ *Insurers Want—and Get—Their Share*
>
> **I**n recent years, there has been a trend toward insurers utilizing outside fund managers for variable annuity products. To offset some of the costs the insurance carrier incurs by having outside funds in its variable annuities (i.e., preparing sales material and advertising related to the fund or maintaining records related to purchases and redemptions of fund shares), insurers have begun asking outside fund managers to help defray some of these costs. Other than a subadvisory arrangement with the fund manager, there are two main ways that fund managers provide revenues to the insurer: (1) by paying the insurer for "subtransfer agent" services and (2) by having the fund's advisor pay the insurer a "reallowance" from its advisory fee profits. Historically, from a regulatory standpoint, the costs that the fund manager was allowed to reimburse to the insurer could not have anything to do with the distribution of the variable annuity *product.* They were limited to expenses involved in distributing the *fund's* shares to variable annuity contract owners. In 1996, however, the SEC agreed to allow fund managers to help pay for some of the distribution costs of a variable annuity through a 12b-1 plan, similar to what occurs today in the retail mutual fund arena.

### No-Load Variable Annuities

Making its way onto the scene is a *no-load variable annuity.* A no-load variable annuity is one with no contingent deferred sales or surrender charge. These no-load products have very low mortality and expense charges, ranging from 50 to 75 basis points of the contract's separate account value. Traditional variable annuities carry mortality and expense charges of 125 to 150 basis points.

One important difference between the new no-load variable products and their traditional counterparts should be emphasized. Most traditional variable annuities today have a general account option that allows the contractholder to direct some of the premiums into a fixed, guaranteed rate alternative, thus reducing his or her risk exposure. Because of the dynamics of such fixed investments, surrender charges are necessary to enable the insurer to invest the money for more than one year. Because the no-load products do not have surrender charges, it is difficult for insurers to offer them with a general (fixed) account option.

### ■ VARIABLE ANNUITY INCOME AND LIQUIDITY OPTIONS

There are a number of ways in which variable annuity owners can use the product for liquidity or to create an income stream. These include free withdrawals, annuitization and systematic withdrawals.

---

**ILL. 6.8 ■** *Typical Features and Options of the Variable Annuity*

**ABC Variable Annuity**

| **Features** | **Separate Accounts** |
|---|---|
| • Annuitization | • Money market |
| • Systematic withdrawal | • Growth fund |
| • Dollar cost averaging | • Bond fund |
| • Unlimited switches | • Global fund |
| • Asset allocation | • Gold fund |
| • Death benefit | • Precious metals fund |
| • Free withdrawals (10% of cumulative premiums) | • Social and environmental fund |
| | • Index fund |
| | • Life cycle fund |

---

### Free Withdrawals

Like fixed annuities, most variable annuities provide liquidity through a free withdrawal feature. In the sample variable annuity shown in Ill. 6.8, the withdrawal feature is defined as 10 percent of the cumulative premiums, any time after the first contract year. Other annuities may allow for 10 percent of the accumulated value of the annuity. Still others may provide access to the cumulative growth within the contract. In other words, any amount earned on the premiums may be withdrawn in any given year.

### Annuitization

Like owners of fixed annuities, variable annuity contractholders have the option of *annuitization*—they can convert the funds in the annuity to an income stream, guaranteed for a certain period of time, for life or for a combination of the two. As discussed in Chapter 3, variable annuitization involves the contractholder selecting an assumed interest or investment rate, known as the AIR. Based on that rate and the payment period, the carrier determines the initial (typically monthly) payment and then converts the payment into units based on the annuity unit value at the time of the initial payment. Subsequent distributions are of the same *number* of annuity units, but the *value* of the units will vary, based on the performance of the underlying separate account. (For a more detailed discussion of variable annuitization, refer to Chapter 3.)

Because the variable annuity houses fixed and separate accounts within the same product, there is an option to create a mixture of a fixed annuity payment and a variable annuity payment. The contractholder simply allocates a dollar amount to the fixed annuity that will result in a guaranteed fixed payment for the term selected by the contractholder, usually life. The balance can be annuitized in the separate account as previously explained.

## Systematic Withdrawals

In addition to annuitization, variable annuity contractholders can use systematic withdrawals to create an income.

Systematic withdrawal from a variable annuity can be accomplished in a number of ways but is most frequently achieved through the liquidation of:

- a specified dollar amount or

- a specified number of accumulation units.

To illustrate the former, the contractholder selects a specific dollar amount that is then systematically withdrawn on a pro rata basis from the various accounts. In the latter case, the withdrawal is made on a pro rata distribution and conversion of accumulation units.

As described earlier, when an individual purchases a separate account variable annuity, he or she actually buys *units* of the separate account, just like a mutual fund. Because most variable annuities are open-ended funds, there is always a market for the units, allowing them to be bought and sold freely at the accumulated unit value. Consequently, when units are systematically distributed instead of dollars, the annuity administrator simply converts units to dollars, and the distribution is made to the contractholder. Obviously, when a contractholder systematically withdraws units, the dollar amount will fluctuate with the unit value. Illustration 6.9 shows how unit value systematic withdrawal works.

## Nursing Home, Hospitalization and Terminal Illness Provisions

Traditionally, variable annuities have not embraced the additional forms of liquidity common to fixed annuity products that allow withdrawals when the annuitant or contractholder enters a nursing home, is hospitalized or is diagnosed with a terminal illness. However, as the variable market has grown and as carriers compete for buyers, some have added these features to their contracts. As is the case with fixed annuity products, a careful review of these provisions is required. There can be limitations that mitigate the benefits.

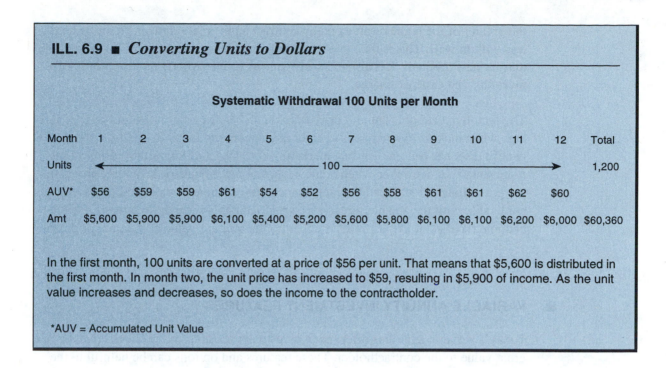

**ILL. 6.9 ■ *Converting Units to Dollars***

**Systematic Withdrawal 100 Units per Month**

| Month | 1 | 2 | 3 | 4 | 5 | 6 | 7 | 8 | 9 | 10 | 11 | 12 | Total |
|---|---|---|---|---|---|---|---|---|---|---|---|---|---|
| Units | ← | | | | | 100 | | | | | | → | 1,200 |
| AUV* | $56 | $59 | $59 | $61 | $54 | $52 | $56 | $58 | $61 | $61 | $62 | $60 | |
| Amt | $5,600 | $5,900 | $5,900 | $6,100 | $5,400 | $5,200 | $5,600 | $5,800 | $6,100 | $6,100 | $6,200 | $6,000 | $60,360 |

In the first month, 100 units are converted at a price of $56 per unit. That means that $5,600 is distributed in the first month. In month two, the unit price has increased to $59, resulting in $5,900 of income. As the unit value increases and decreases, so does the income to the contractholder.

*AUV = Accumulated Unit Value

## Death Benefit

By virtue of their classification as an insurance product, variable annuities have certain inherent guarantees. Obviously, one guarantee is the return on and benefits from the fixed account if the product has a fixed account option. (Some do not.) Regardless, all variable annuities have some type of *death benefit* that is payable if the annuitant dies before payments begin. Depending on the provisions of the contract, the death benefit will be defined according to one of the following. Some contracts allow the buyer to choose how the death benefit will be defined.

**Traditional death benefit.** The traditional death benefit under a variable annuity is the greater of the annuity account value at death, or premiums paid less withdrawals taken through age 85. After age 85, it is simply the account value.

**Compounded death benefit reset.** Under this approach, the death benefit is defined as the greater of the premium paid and accumulated at a fixed rate of interest (e.g., 4 percent) or the value of the annuity account at death. Some insurers lock in the value of the contract periodically to insure that the owner receives some value from the market gains.

**Ratcheted death benefit reset.** With this type of reset, the death benefit is the greater of the account value or the premiums paid, less withdrawals; however, the account value is periodically reset as described above. Under a six-year reset, for example, the insurer will reset the death benefit every six years at the greater of the account value at that time or premiums paid less withdrawals.

**Highest anniversary value reset.** Under this approach, the death benefit is reset annually based on the highest anniversary value. This means that the death benefit is the greater of the highest value on any contract anniversary date or premiums paid, less withdrawals. This is the newest form of death benefit reset and is the most popular for new products. It is also expensive and as noted earlier, may result in a higher mortality and expense charge.

The fact that a variable annuity provides a death benefit gives it a significant advantage when making comparisons to other investment products. In addition, the death benefit reset has become a strong marketing and sales tool for variable annuity sales representatives. However, when reviewing a contract's death benefit reset provision, the practitioner should read the language carefully. Some of these resets are only applicable until the annuitant reaches a specified age, at which time the resets may become fixed as of the last reset or revert to the account value at the time of death.

## ■ VARIABLE ANNUITY INVESTMENT FEATURES

Today's variable annuities offer many investment features and funds that can be of great value to the contractholder. These features and options can be helpful to the insurance professional in tailoring a variable annuity to meet the specific needs of the future contractholder.

### Dollar Cost Averaging

*Dollar cost averaging* (DCA) is a method of purchasing variable units within the variable annuity in order to take advantage of regular, level investments over a period of time. By using DCA, contractholders can keep their average cost below the market, employing the age-old adage of "buy low, sell high." Only with DCA, it is "buy more when prices are low and buy less when prices are high."

Illustration 6.10 shows how DCA works. The contractholder has committed to investing $500 per month. Each month, the $500 may buy a different number of units based on the accumulated unit value. In the first month, $500 will buy 50 units at a price of $10 per unit. As the price goes up in month four to $20 per unit, the $500 only buys 25 units. By this process, the contractholder automatically limits purchasing at the "high" mark by buying fewer units. This illustration shows how DCA works in an "up" market and in a "down" market. During the "up" market, the average cost per unit is $15.98 ($3,000 ÷ 187.7). The average price over the six-month period is $17. During the "down" market, the average cost per unit is $14.35, somewhat less than the average unit price of $15.17. With DCA, the average cost is always less than the average price.

In the variable annuity, DCA is accomplished by depositing money into the money market account. The insurance company or its administrator then systematically transfers a fixed dollar amount into the separate account options chosen by the contractholder. In a minor variation, some insurers move the money from the fixed

## ILL. 6.10 ■ *Dollar Cost Averaging*

| How DCA Works in an "Up" Market | | | | | How DCA Works in a "Down" Market | | | |
|---|---|---|---|---|---|---|---|---|
| Month | Deposit | Unit Price | Units Bought | | Month | Deposit | Unit Price | Units Bought |
| 1 | $ 500 | $ 10 | 50.00 | | 1 | $ 500 | $ 20 | 25.00 |
| 2 | $ 500 | $ 15 | 33.33 | | 2 | $ 500 | $ 18 | 27.78 |
| 3 | $ 500 | $ 18 | 27.78 | | 3 | $ 500 | $ 16 | 31.25 |
| 4 | $ 500 | $ 20 | 25.00 | | 4 | $ 500 | $ 15 | 33.33 |
| 5 | $ 500 | $ 21 | 23.81 | | 5 | $ 500 | $ 10 | 50.00 |
| 6 | $ 500 | $ 18 | 27.78 | | 6 | $ 500 | $ 12 | 41.67 |
| | $3,000 | $ 17 | 187.70 | | | $3,000 | $ 15.17 | 209.03 |
| | | Avg. Price | Total Units | | | | Avg. Price | Total Units |

Average cost per unit = $15.98       Average cost per unit = $14.35

account to the separate account options instead of using the money market fund. This is done without a market value adjustment.

### Fund Switches

*Fund switches* or *transfers* are an integral part of the variable annuity. This is the mechanism that allows the contractholder to move money from one fund option to another fund option with the ease of a phone call. Typically, insurers allow contractholders to make a number of moves or switches with no charge; after a certain number, however, the contractholder may be assessed a charge. In addition, switches can be made from variable accounts to the fixed accounts and from the fixed accounts to the variable accounts. Remember that transfers made from the fixed account to the variable account may be subject to the market value adjustment as described earlier in this chapter.

### "Sweeps"

There are a number of people who buy variable annuities but are afraid to jump into the market with both feet. For those individuals and for those who, because of the risk, would not otherwise consider the purchase of a variable annuity, several insurance companies now offer an easy way to get into the market. The contractholder deposits his or her initial premium into the variable annuity's general account. Then periodically, the insurer "sweeps" the account interest into the separate account based on an allocation specified by the contractholder. This approach minimizes the risk and allows the buyer to gradually become accustomed to the separate account investing and market risk.

## Asset Allocation

One way for contractholders to take advantage of the switching provisions within the variable annuity is to use the insurer's *asset allocation* program, if offered. Asset allocation is a method of letting the experts manage the contractholder's money. When the contractholder elects this option, the company's asset managers move the money for the contractholder and/or change the allocation percentage for future deposits.

Contractholders can designate part or all of their accounts to be moved and spread as the money manager sees fit. Theoretically, if the asset manager thinks interest rates are going to move up and the market is going to move down, he or she will shift a large percentage, perhaps even all, of the contractholder's money into the money market account. If, on the other hand, the manager feels that a more balanced approach is required, the assets will be allocated accordingly.

Some variable annuities have set up their asset allocation as a separate investment account. In those cases, the monies are not transferred. Instead the asset manager simply buys and sells within the fund portfolio to create the desired mix based on market conditions.

## Portfolio Rebalancing

With advances in technology have come better and more capable administrative systems for insurers. These enhanced systems allow companies to offer new features and services that previously were not available or were too expensive. *Portfolio rebalancing* is one such feature. The concept behind portfolio rebalancing is that over time, the initial allocation of funds within a variable annuity becomes altered or unbalanced as a result of performance. What this ends up doing is changing the portfolio's orientation or configuration toward the amount of risk the contractholder wants to assume. In theory, the older we get, the less risk we want to take. In practice, without portfolio rebalancing, just the opposite occurs.

Let's look at a simple example. Joe is 45 years old and invests $100,000 in a variable annuity. He elects to allocate $50,000 into a stable blue-chip equity subaccount and $50,000 into a highly speculative international growth subaccount. After 10 years, the blue-chip fund has grown an average of 8 percent a year and is now valued at $107,946. The speculative international growth fund has grown at an average of 18 percent a year and is now worth $261,692. Joe is happy because he now has more than $350,000. But the configuration of his investment is now way out of alignment: over 70 percent of his assets are in a subaccount that no longer meets his risk tolerance needs. Portfolio rebalancing automatically adjusts or rebalances the portfolio to match the original allocation. In this example, portfolio rebalancing would adjust

Joe's account so that 50 percent of the assets are in the blue-chip subaccount and 50 percent are in the speculative growth subaccount.

Portfolio rebalancing reduces the risk of the separate account; however, it should be done in conjunction with an annual review to make sure that future allocations are consistent with the client's ever-changing objectives and risk tolerance.

## ■ TYPES OF VARIABLE ANNUITY SUBACCOUNTS

Today there are thousands of mutual funds, with more being introduced each day. This means that it has become more difficult for buyers—as well as practitioners—to choose an appropriate fund or funds for a variable annuity. There are variable products today that have over 35 subaccount options in the separate account. Though many might argue that too many funds can confuse a potential buyer (and prompt closer scrutiny by the IRS), others maintain that a variety of investment choices gives the consumer a better opportunity to match his or her investment objectives with those of the underlying funds. Let's look at just a few of the different types of fund options that are currently available on the market. (Keep in mind that the technical term for the options within an insurer's separate account is "subaccounts." These subaccounts are routinely called "funds," but they should never be referred to as mutual funds.)

### Money Market Accounts

A *money market* fund invests in very secure, short-term investments. Typically, maturities do not exceed one year. The fund usually consists of CDs, Treasury bills and commercial paper, which are short-term notes usually issued by large, financially secure corporations. Because of the short duration of the portfolio, interest rates on money market funds are usually low when compared to other, long-term investments.

### Growth Accounts

A *growth* account is one that exclusively or primarily invests in common stocks of corporations. Depending on the objectives of the particular growth fund, you may find very conservative stocks or perhaps some more risky issues, if the fund is geared toward aggressive gains. Again depending on the objectives, some growth funds are aimed at the more aggressive risk taker while others seek more conservative capital gains with some dividend distribution to provide limited income. Some funds may even target smaller companies for better growth.

## Bond Accounts

*Bond* accounts tend to be attractive to those individuals seeking income from the variable annuity. As their name implies, bond funds invest exclusively or primarily in debt securities. As is the case with growth funds, there are a variety of degrees of risk. High-risk bond funds purchase lower grade debt security than a more traditional bond fund, which may buy higher quality, lower yielding bonds.

Bond funds are subject to interest rate risk much more so than stock/growth funds. As interest rates rise, the stock market may or may not respond negatively; but the value of a bond fund will go down and corresponding income will be more susceptible to inflation.

## Global Accounts

*Global* and *international* accounts are very popular today. Global funds seek to buy debt and equity issues from other prospering or developing nations, in addition to those of the United States. A variation of these funds are international funds, which invest all of their funds outside of the United States. Many advisors believe that the diversification offered by global and international funds will be very desirable for long-term investors.

As this market continues to mature and grow, new variations of these funds have become available. One example is the global government bond funds that only invest in foreign government debt issues. Contractholders should be aware that most of the global or international funds contain higher than average management fees and expenses.

## Precious Metals Accounts

As the name suggests, *precious metals* accounts comprise equity and debt instruments of companies involved in gold and other precious metals.

## Social and Environmental Accounts

These types of funds "screen" the investments purchased by the asset managers, depending on the fund objectives. Some funds screen for social causes and others focus on social, environmental or combinations of causes. These funds invest in companies that are determined to be socially and/or environmentally responsible, because (in theory) these companies will be in a better position within their respective markets.

### Index Accounts

A new fund offered by a handful of mutual fund companies is an *index fund*. The index fund attempts to "mirror" a major index—such as the S&P 500—and match its gains and losses. In a variation of this strategy, some insurers are including an index option in their general account, providing the contractholder with both an index return and a minimum guarantee of interest.

### Life Cycle Funds

Just beginning to develop on the variable annuity scene, *life cycle funds* focus on the consumer's life cycle stage and are defined by age and lifestyle. There are generally three types of funds, oriented to various financial stages in a person's life:

1. the accumulation stage (ages 25 to 45);

2. the preservation stage (ages 45 to 60); and

3. the distribution stage (ages 60 and over).

The underlying portfolios of these funds are structured to address the various needs at the specific stage.

### ■ LICENSING AND REGISTRATION

Unlike the fixed annuity, the variable annuity requires that the producer not only have an insurance license but also a securities license. (The securities license required is the Series 6, which covers variable annuities and mutual funds.) In addition, some states require a variable annuity insurance license.

NASD regulations typically require that a practitioner house his or her securities license with one broker-dealer. The broker-dealer will then offer the practitioner variable annuities from the insurers with whom the broker-dealer has contracted to do business.

With so much growth and activity in the variable annuity arena, it is inevitable that the industry will run into compliance and market conduct issues as they pertain to consumers who are not familiar with variable products. An individual who exchanges a fixed annuity for a variable annuity may not fully realize the risks he or she has assumed. The practitioner is responsible for addressing such issues. The practitioner should make sure that the buyer reads and understands the prospectus. In addition, the practitioner is well advised to follow up in writing with prospects and clients to ensure that they understand the risks associated with the variable product.

■ **SUMMARY**

In this chapter we took a look at variable annuities—how they allow contractholders to direct the investment of their premium dollars, the costs associated with these products and how those costs are expressed. We discussed typical investment features and investment funds available for variable annuities. How variable annuities should be "positioned" in the market and how they compare to mutual funds, an investment with which they are inevitably compared, are the subjects of the next chapter.

■ **CHAPTER 6 QUESTIONS FOR REVIEW**

1. To sell variable annuities, a practitioner must be licensed with the NASD.

   *True* or *False*

2. The separate account is part of the general account of the insurance company.

   *True* or *False*

3. The market value adjustment protects the insurer against losses should a variable annuity contractholder wish to move money from the separate account to the general account.

   *True* or *False*

4. The SEC requires that all variable annuity sales materials sent to a consumer be accompanied by a current prospectus.

   *True* or *False*

5. All of the following are separate account investment options EXCEPT:

   a. money market funds.
   b. bond funds.
   c. guaranteed one-year investment rates.
   d. global equity funds.

6. Which of the following describes the traditional death benefit provision in a variable annuity contract?

   a. The greater of the contract's highest account value on any anniversary date or premiums paid
   b. The lesser of the contract's account value at death or premiums paid, less withdrawals
   c. The greater of the contract's account value, reset every five years, or premiums paid
   d. The greater of the contract's account value at death or premiums paid, less withdrawals

# 7

# Variable Annuities and Mutual Funds

A s you learned in Chapter 6, the separate account of a variable annuity is made up of many subaccounts. These subaccounts are similar in form and substance to mutual funds. Given this similarity and the fact that variable annuities and mutual funds are used for similar purposes, comparisons are inevitably made. Unfortunately, comparisons by the media are often flawed because they tend to focus on expenses instead of performance. Comparisons should be based on performance. Obviously, expenses affect performance, but they are only one factor. All factors must be considered and that is what performance does.

The purpose of this chapter is to outline the differences and similarities between annuities and mutual funds. For a practitioner to make appropriate product and investment recommendations, it's imperative that he or she understand both products.

■ ■ ■ ■ ■

## ■ DEFINITIONS AND ASSUMPTIONS

To make a complete and fair comparison, we need to start with some underlying definitions and assumptions. First, the definitions.

### Mutual Funds

Mutual funds can be long-term or short-term savings vehicles, and they may or may not be used for retirement. For purposes of comparison, we will only evaluate the mutual funds as they are used for long-term retirement savings. Unfortunately, as you'll learn later, most investors don't understand how to use mutual funds for retirement.

There are basically three ways an investor gets a return on a nonqualified mutual fund investment: dividends, capital gains generated by the fund and capital gains generated by selling or liquidating shares. For simplicity, we'll designate gains generated by the fund as *internal* and those generated by liquidation on the part of the shareholder as *external*. Dividends and internal gains are reported as income to the shareholder each year and are taxed accordingly. External capital gains are taxed only at the time of sale by the shareholder. If the shares sold were held longer than a year, then the shareholder enjoys long-term capital gains treatment, which may mean a lower tax rate. In addition, mutual funds take a stepped-up cost basis at death. This means that when the shareholder dies, the cost basis of the investment is the market value as of the date of death; the beneficiary is not taxed on any unrecognized external capital gains. (Keep in mind that this tax advantage only applies to external capital gains realized at death, as taxes have been paid along the way on dividends and internal capital gains.)

## Variable Annuities

Now to the variable annuity. Annuities enjoy tax deferral because they are long-term retirement savings vehicles. This is the primary purpose they serve and, for the most part, it is the reason most people purchase them and hold them for the long term. You'll see the significance of this in the performance comparison.

As you've learned, annuities generate no current taxable income. No taxable income is generated for dividends, none for internal gain and none for external gain. In fact, not only is no taxable income created for external gains on fund switches within a variable annuity, no taxable income is generated when the contractholder switches from one variable annuity to another. (See Chapter 11.) With a variable annuity, a taxable event is created only when monies are removed from the contract.

## Assumptions

Now that the definitions are clear, let's look at the assumptions. To make an effective comparison, we need to make reasonable assumptions. These are outlined below.

### Assumptions for Mutual Fund and VA Comparison

- Use five-year historical returns for variable annuity subaccounts and mutual funds; period ending December 31, 1995. (Source: Morningstar. See Ill. 7.1.)

- Use five-year historical differences in variable annuity subaccounts and mutual fund returns. (See Ill. 7.1.)

- Compare most commonly used load methods (contingent deferred sales charge for variable annuity and front-end load for mutual fund).

- 30 percent of mutual fund distributions (internal turnover) are taxed as long-term capital gains.

- 25 percent of mutual fund gains are deferred until external turnover.

- External fund turnover occurs every four years (industry average).

- Goal of both variable annuity and mutual fund is to generate maximum retirement income.

- Buyer invests $100,000 at age 50, accumulates for 15 years, retires at age 65, then takes a level distribution of income until age 80, at which time the account is depleted.

- Ordinary income tax rate of 42 percent, which includes federal and state taxes and the effects of the phaseout of deductions and exemptions. (For high-income individuals in high-tax states, a more accurate rate would be in excess of 50 percent.)

- Capital gains tax rate of 31 percent (includes federal and state tax).

- Contingent deferred sales charge for the annuity: 6 percent, 5 percent, 4 percent, 3 percent, 2 percent, 1 percent.

- 4 percent front-end mutual fund load.

---

### ILL. 7.1 ■ *Variable Annuity Subaccounts vs. Mutual Funds*

#### PERFORMANCE

#### Average Compound Annual Returns for Five Years Ending 12/31/95

|  | Annuity | Mutual Fund | Annuity Advantage |
|---|---|---|---|
| U.S. Equity | 17.19% | 16.64% | + .55% |
| Bonds | 10.29% | 8.27% | + 2.02% |
| International Equity* | 8.43% | 10.54% | − 2.11% |

Returns are net of all fund fees and expenses, all subaccount fees and expenses and all mortality and expense charges.

*Note: At this time, there are very few international subaccounts in variable annuities; therefore, the statistical significance of the international comparison is questionable.

*Source:* Morningstar

## ■ RESULTS

Here are the results of the comparison. The first shows the results of a variable annuity and mutual fund when 100 percent of the assets of each are invested in equities (Ill. 7.2 shows a graph of these results); the second shows the results when the assets of each are invested 50 percent in equities and 50 percent in bonds. Note that all results are after accounting for fund fees, subaccount fees and mortality and expense charges.

### 100% U.S. Equity

|  | Annuity | Mutual Fund |
| --- | --- | --- |
| Initial deposit: | $100,00 | $96,000* |
| Account value at 15 years: | $1,079,800 | $458,800 |
| After-tax annual income for years 16 thru 30: | $104,000 | $53,700 |
| Account value at year 30: | $0 | $0 |
| Annual annuity advantage: | $50,300 | |

*After accounting for 4 percent front-end load

### 50% Equity/50% Bond

|  | Annuity | Mutual Fund |
| --- | --- | --- |
| Initial deposit: | $100,000 | $96,000* |
| Account value at 15 years: | $689,800 | $313,700 |
| After-tax annual income for years 16 thru 30: | $59,300 | $32,500 |
| Account value at year 30: | $0 | $0 |
| Annual annuity advantage: | $26,800 | |

*After accounting for 4 percent front-end load

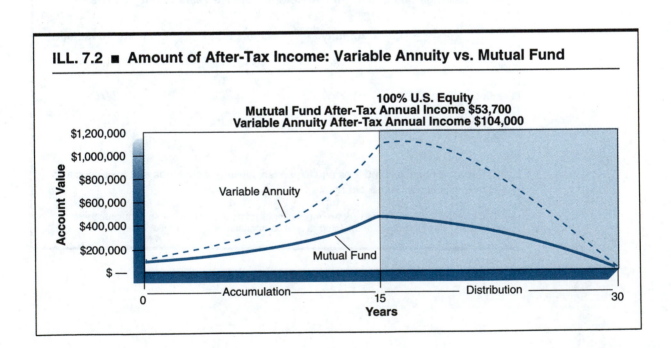

**ILL. 7.2 ■ Amount of After-Tax Income: Variable Annuity vs. Mutual Fund**

Here's another way of looking at the results. In this comparison, we'll match the after-tax payout of the variable annuity to that of the mutual fund and see how much longer the payout of the variable annuity will last. Again, the first shows the comparison of a variable annuity and a mutual fund invested 100 percent in equities (Ill. 7.3 shows a graph of these results); the second is a comparison of these two products invested 50 percent in equities and 50 percent in bonds.

### 100% U.S. Equity

|  | Annuity | Mutual Fund |
|---|---|---|
| Initial deposit: | $100,000 | $96,000* |
| Account value at 15 years: | $1,079,800 | $458,800 |
| After-tax annual income for years 16 thru 30: | $104,000 | $104,000 |
| Account value at year 30: | $0 | $0 |
| Number of years of payout: | 15 | 5 |
| Annuity advantage in years: | 10 | |

*After accounting for 4 percent front-end load

### 50% Equity/50% Bond

|  | Annuity | Mutual Fund |
|---|---|---|
| Initial deposit: | $100,000 | $96,000* |
| Account value at 15 years: | $689,800 | $313,700 |
| After-tax annual income for years 16 thru 30: | $59,300 | $59,300 |
| Number of years of payout: | 15 | 6 |
| Annuity advantage in years: | 9 | |

*After accounting for 4 percent front-end load

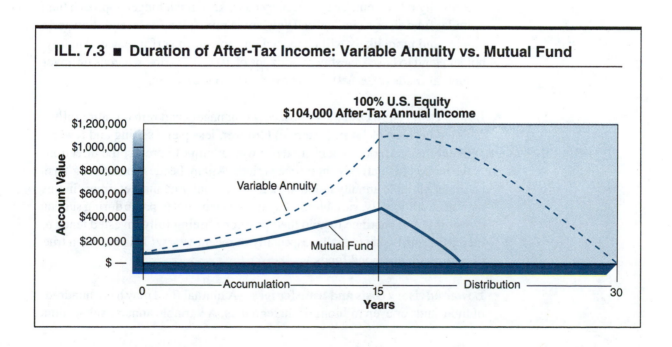

ILL. 7.3 ■ Duration of After-Tax Income: Variable Annuity vs. Mutual Fund

## ■ THE ANALYSIS

Based on a performance comparison, we see that the variable annuity more than holds its own to the mutual fund. Now that we've seen the results, it's time to get an appreciation for why the results are what they are. Many analysts simply evaluate variable annuities as being more expensive by the amount of the mortality and expense fee. In other words, these analysts determine the performance of variable annuity subaccounts by subtracting the mortality and expense fee (which averages approximately 1.35 percent of the subaccount balance) from mutual funds returns. This would mean that the subaccounts would always be at a disadvantage compared to mutual funds. This type of analysis would be fine *if it were valid*. But it isn't valid, as Ill. 7.1 proves.

What accounts for the fact that subaccounts have better performance with higher fees? Before we address that question, let's review what the extra costs are. As noted in Chapter 6, variable annuity insurers charge additional fees for mortality and expenses. These fees range from .4 percent to 1.75 percent of the subaccount balance, with the average being 1.35 percent. Some analysts assert that this is the charge for tax deferral. That is not correct. There is no charge for tax deferral. Tax deferral is granted, without cost, by the federal government to annuities as long-term retirement savings vehicles. There is no cost . . . period.

So, if tax deferral is free, what costs 1.35 percent? This is the cost to the insurer for the mortality risk of the specific death benefit and other expenses. This being the case, then the subaccount must perform 1.35 percent better than the mutual fund each year. How is it able to do this? Following are the reasons that variable annuity subaccounts not only make up for mortality, but can actually outperform mutual funds:

- **Longer-term investment horizons**—Subaccount managers know that 100 percent of the monies in their accounts are destined for a long-term horizon, specifically retirement. Therefore, they can take a much longer approach than a similar fund since a similar fund will have a mix of long-term and short-term monies and more likely will be judged on short-term performance. Annuity holders tend to have investment horizons of 10 to 15 years, whereas turnover of mutual funds (external) occurs every two to four years.

- **Lower cash requirements**—Subaccount managers can remain more fully invested because of lower (external) turnover, less panic selling and fewer market timers. Market timers are those who attempt to predict the direction of the market in relatively short time periods. Again, because of the long-term nature of variable annuity holders, there are virtually no market timers in this market. Additionally, variable annuity holders tend not to panic during sudden downturns and continue to hold their positions. Being fully invested tends to increase returns substantially, especially in recent years. (This has been true of both stock and bond funds.)

- **Lower advisory costs and transfer fees**—A mutual fund may have hundreds of thousands or even millions of shareholders. A variable annuity subaccount has only one shareholder—the insurer. Therefore, the subaccount has to carry only the expenses associated with that one shareholder. This means substantial savings. Admittedly, not all of these savings are passed on to the policyholder. Even though there is only one shareholder, there are still thousands of policyholders and these policyholders have to be serviced. But instead of being serviced by the fund, they are serviced by the insurer. Ultimately, this serves to mitigate the effects of the 1.35 mortality and expense charge and substantially increases overall performance relative to funds.

- **No tax consequences for trades**—Mutual fund managers are consistently attempting to increase the after-tax return of their fund. This means they must be cognizant of any trades that produce internal capital gains. Additionally, they may pass over potentially high performing stocks or bonds that generate high dividends. Subaccount managers need not worry about these issues. They are free to make any purchase or sale they wish, because these trades generate no tax current tax consequences for the policyholder.

- **Contractual fee limits**—Generally subaccount fees, including mortality and expense, are limited by the terms of the contract. The starting fees typically are equal to the lifetime maximums. This is not true of mutual funds. Most

---

**ILL. 7.4 ■ *Variable Annuities and Mutual Funds: Comparison of Features***

| Variable Annuities | Mutual Funds |
|---|---|
| • Tax deferred | • Gains and income currently taxable |
| • Ordinary income treatment | • Capital gains treatment |
| • Exclusion ratio available | • Stepped-up cost basis |
| • Long-term savings | • Long-term or short-term savings |
| • 10 percent pre-59½ withdrawal penalty | |
| • No stepped-up cost basis | |
| • Probate avoidance | |
| • Death benefit | |
| • General (fixed) account usually available | |
| • Lifetime income available | |

fund fees can be increased by vote of the trustees. It's too early to say what the long-term impact of this difference may be, but it has the potential to be significant.

Combined, these reasons serve to make the positive difference with variable annuity subaccounts. In addition, variable annuity policyholders have a death benefit and, typically, the flexibility to invest in a general account as well. It should be also be noted that many of the advantages mentioned here also pertain to qualified applications. Because tax deferral is free, one need only consider other features, benefits and performance to determine if qualified monies fit in the annuity. You'll find that they often do and are so used about 50 percent of the time.

## ■ SUMMARY

In this chapter we outlined the differences and similarities between variable annuities and mutual funds. To make proper comparisons, one must have a complete understanding of both products. This understanding seems to be simple for all products but the annuity. If the practitioner takes the time to understand the proper application and position of the annuity in the retirement planning arena and make appropriate product comparisons, consumer awareness and understanding will increase as well, ultimately benefiting all.

## ■ CHAPTER 7 QUESTIONS FOR REVIEW

1. Variable annuities tend to have shorter investment horizons than mutual funds.

   *True* or *False*

2. Mutual funds tend to have lower advisory costs and transfer fees than variable annuities.

   *True* or *False*

3. All of the following are taxable, EXCEPT:

   a. dividends paid on a mutual fund held by the owner.
   b. internal gains on a mutual fund held by the owner.
   c. dividends paid on a variable annuity held by the owner.
   d. internal gains on a variable annuity upon surrender.

4. When comparing variable annuities and mutual funds for retirement planning purposes, the practitioner should focus on

    a. expenses.
    b. liquidity.
    c. performance.
    d. mortality cost.

# 8

# Annuity Benefits

I n this chapter, we will discuss the five primary benefits of the annuity and how they have shaped the development of the market. To be successful in the presentation and sale of annuities, the practitioner must understand how these benefits help solve consumer problems and meet consumer needs. These key benefits are: *safety, tax deferral, yield, liquidity* and *probate avoidance*.

■ ■ ■ ■ ■

## ■ SAFETY: AN INSURANCE INDUSTRY STANDARD

The principle reason that individuals purchase an annuity is *safety*. Because of this fundamental need for safety, the insurance industry has gone to great lengths to protect the contractholder and guarantee his or her investment. As a result, only once in the industry's history have annuity contractholders lost money. In this first section, we will review the reasons why the annuity is such a safe investment and how insurers are able to make the guarantees they do.

### Reserving

The guarantee of annuity principal is grounded in the *legal reserve system*. The legal reserve system, developed specifically to protect contractholders (and insurance policyowners) through prudent asset management and accounting practices, has been in existence since the beginning of the 20th century.

At the heart of the legal reserve system are the statutory reserves that every insurance company must establish to protect its contracts and contractholders. The statutory reserve that the company is required to establish is based on the contractual provisions of its annuity or life contracts.

Insurance company reserving and accounting are extremely complicated and technical subjects and in-depth coverage is beyond the scope of this text. However, a basic knowledge of the system can be helpful when making relative comparisons of the annuity to other investments that your clients or prospects may be considering. One of the most important points that should be made is the difference between *capital, surplus* and *reserves* and how they relate to the safety of the annuity contractholder.

### Capital and Surplus

Capital and surplus are, in essence, the net worth of the insurance company. Generally speaking, they are the assets of the insurer minus its liabilities. To maintain the integrity of the reserve system, companies may periodically increase reserves in recognition of losses or potential losses in their investment portfolios. Also, the company uses capital and surplus to invest in the writing of new business and relies on them as a safety buffer for emergencies. As a whole, the capital and surplus of the insurance industry as a percentage of assets is currently about 8 percent.

### Reserves

Reserves are liabilities to the insurance company, representing funds set aside to meet the company's contractual obligations. They are invested by the insurer and backed by assets of the company. Reserves are only subject to the creditors of the company after all contractholder claims have been resolved. Obviously, this provides great safety to the contractholder, whose claim is placed ahead of bondholders and shareholders.

When overseen by state regulators, the balance between surplus and reserves provides a remarkable degree of safety, unparalleled in the investment world. Under careful monitoring and management by the NAIC, the insurance industry remains one of an elite group of industries not under the control of the federal government. This is, in large part, a result of the efficient solvency system currently in place.

### Risk-Based Capital

As the investment side of the insurance industry grew, regulators quickly learned that the existing standards of measuring a company's solvency were somewhat antiquated. New investment products were increasingly difficult to qualify and quantify and old standards simply had no way of addressing these new products. With the demise of Executive Life Insurance Company, First Capital Life Insurance Company and Fidelity Bankers Life Insurance Company, regulators realized that changes had to be made. The most significant of these was the adoption of the "*risk-based capital*" model.

Risk-based capital (RBC) is a method of measuring the capital needs of an insurer based on the types of risk the company assumes. These risks are categorized into four groups: mortality risk, asset risk, interest rate risk and general business risk. Ultimately, the insurer is evaluated on the amount of capital in relation to amount of risk.

## ILL. 8.1 ■ *Risk-Based Capital Model—Four Categories of Risk*

| | |
|---|---|
| Mortality risk: | The risk that claims might exceed projections because of adverse mortality and morbidity experience |
| Asset risk: | The risk that an insurer's long-term assets, such as bonds and mortgage, may go into default |
| Interest rate risk: | The risk of losses because of interest rate fluctuations |
| General business risk: | The risk of business failure, whether of the immediate carrier or another (the latter requiring a state guaranty fund assessment) |

Certain ratios are created and insurers that fall below certain benchmarks are subject to review.

When evaluating the financial stability of an insurance company, risk-based capital is simply one tool that regulators use. It is not an end-all measurement. Risk-based capital comparisons should not be made between insurers because RBC numbers do not tell a company's entire story. Other tools, such as claims-paying ratings, should be used in addition to RBC numbers when practitioners evaluate insurers.

### Investment Regulation

Just as there are laws insurers must follow to protect their investments, there are also regulations that monitor and restrict the investments themselves. In light of earlier insolvencies among annuity carriers, the NAIC moved to limit the types of investments that have caused trouble for carriers. There are now strict limits on affiliated investments, or investments that an insurer makes in itself or in its subsidiary companies (recall the case of Baldwin-United), and below investment-grade bonds (junk bonds). New regulations are being considered to better contain problem mortgages and real estate. The significance of well-managed annuity investments—and how insurers accomplish this—is discussed in Chapter 10.

### Rating Agencies

Another measure of safety for the annuity buyer and those who sell annuity products is provided by independent *rating agencies*. Over the past century, there has been one dominant company that has rated insurance companies: A.M. Best. Typically, the practitioner has looked to A.M. Best to provide critical information regarding the solvency and profitability of the various insurance companies. Historically, A.M. Best did not charge a fee for its service, nor did it charge the consumer for the

## ILL. 8.2 ■ *Insurance Company Ratings*

| A.M. Best | | Standard & Poor's | | Moody's | | Duff & Phelp's | |
|---|---|---|---|---|---|---|---|
| *Rating* | *Explanation* | *Rating* | *Explanation* | *Rating* | *Explanation* | *Rating* | *Explanation* |
| A++, A+ | Superior; very strong ability to meet obligations. | AAA | Superior; highest safety. | Aaa | Exceptional security. | AAA | Highest claims-paying ability; negligible risk. |
| A, A– | Excellent; strong ability to meet obligations. | AA | Excellent financial security. | Aa | Excellent security. | AA+, AA, AA– | Very high claims-paying ability; moderate risk. |
| B++, B+ | Very good; strong ability to meet obligations. | A | Good financial security. | A | Good security. | A+, A, A– | High claims-paying ability; variable risk over time. |
| B, B– | Good; adequate ability to meet obligations. | BBB | Adequate financial security. | Baa | Adequate security. | | |
| C++, C+ | Fair; reasonable ability to meet obligations. | BB | Adequate financial security; ability to meet obligations may not be adequate for long-term policies. | Ba | Questionable security; moderate ability to meet obligations. | BBB+, BBB, BBB– | Below average claims-paying ability; considerable variability in risk over time. |
| C, C– | Marginal; currently has ability to meet obligations. | B | Currently able to meet obligations, but highly vulnerable to adverse conditions. | B | Poor security. | BB+, BB, BB– | Uncertain claims-paying ability. |
| D | Below minimum standards. | CCC | Questionable ability to meet obligations. | Caa | Very poor security; elements of danger regarding payment of obligations. | CCC | Substantial claims-paying ability risk; likely to be placed under state supervision. |
| E | Under state supervision. | CC, C | May not be meeting obligations; vulnerable to liquidation. | Ca | Extremely poor security; may be in default. | | |
| F | In liquidation. | D | Under an order of liquidation. | C | Lowest security. | DD | Under an order of liquidation. |

company's analysis. Insurance companies have always supplied their policyowners and contractholders with these reports as a marketing tool.

In the late 1980s, as the industry grew more and more complex financially, A.M. Best found that the time and resources required to properly evaluate an insurance company were becoming prohibitive. As a result, Best started charging insurance companies a fee for its rating. Shortly thereafter, A.M. Best began to receive fairly stiff competition from two other companies whose primary function is to rate corporate bonds. In 1986, those two companies, Moody's and Standard & Poor's, began evaluating insurance companies and assigning what they called "claims-paying ratings." These new ratings coincided with their own particular nomenclature that they used to rate corporate bonds. In fact, Standard & Poor's is the only rating agency to have two separate rating services: a qualified solvency rating and a claims-paying rating. Another rating agency that provides claims-paying ratings is Duff & Phelps. Illustration 8.2 shows a relative comparison between these major rating agencies.

In general, the rating agencies attempt to evaluate the current ability of an insurer to pay its claims. A number of quantitative and qualitative tests are conducted to make this determination. Ratings are typically assigned for a one-year period; however, each of the agencies reserves the right to change a rating at any time based on the operating results of the insurer.

The point of this discussion is to emphasize that the insurance industry remains one of the most highly regulated and scrutinized industries in the country. In addition to all of the state regulatory requirements, the industry must also contend with the growing debate over federal regulation of the industry. All of this attention and regulation provides the consumer with a tremendous amount of information to evaluate the insurance industry and its safety.

## State Guaranty Funds

Each of the 50 states has enacted legislation to protect the contractholders of that state should an insurance company be faced with insolvency. This legislation has resulted in the creation of 50 *guaranty funds*, required by the state but funded by the insurance companies that are admitted to do business in that state. Most state guaranty funds assess their admitted insurers an extra charge to cover any carrier insolvencies within the state. Different states have different limits of protection. Illustration 8.3 shows all of the state guaranty funds, and the amount that the fund will guarantee to any one contractholder within those states.

It is important to emphasize that these state guaranty funds provide the contractholder with protection without federal or state funding. All guaranty associations are funded by insurance companies and administered by the states. However, practitioners should check with their states to confirm limitations and to determine whether or not they even have the right to disclose the existence of the guaranty fund. Many states do not allow disclosure of guaranty fund information to potential contractholders because they do not want insurers and producers to rely on the fund and its guarantees when designing and marketing products. To do so could lead to abuse of the guaranty associations.

## Safety of Principal

*Safety of principal* in any investment is affected by a number of risks. Interest rates, business cycles, price levels, consumer confidence—any or all of these things can affect the value of an investment. *Asset value fluctuation* is the adjustment that occurs in the value of any asset as outside influences, such as interest rates and business risk, affect the underlying market value of that investment. However, regardless

## ILL 8.3 ■ *Life and Health Insurance Guaranty Associations' Limits of Liability*

| | Death benefits per individual | Life benefits cash values per individual | Cash values per individual | PV of annuities per individual (includes cash values) | Aggregate benefits per individual (all life, health and annuities) |
|---|---|---|---|---|---|
| Alaska | $300,000 | $100,000 | | $100,000 | $300,000 |
| Alabama | | | $100,000 | | |
| Arizona | | 100,000 | | 100,000 | 300,000 |
| Arkansas | 100,000 | 100,000 | | 100,000 | 300,000 |
| California* | 250,000 | 100,000 | | 100,000 | 250,000 |
| Colorado | 300,000 | 100,000 | | 100,000 | 300,000 |
| Connecticut | 300,000 | 100,000 | | 100,000 | 300,000 |
| Delaware | 300,000 | 100,000 | | 100,000 | 300,000 |
| Florida | | | 100,000 | | 300,000 |
| Georgia | | | 100,000 | | 300,000 |
| Hawaii | 300,000 | 100,000 | | 100,000 | 300,000 |
| Idaho | | | 100,000 | | 300,000 |
| Illinois | 300,000 | 100,000 | | 100,000 | 300,000 |
| Indiana | | | 100,000 | | 300,000 |
| Iowa | | | 100,000 | | 300,000 |
| Kansas | 300,000 | 100,000 | | 100,000 | 300,000 |
| Kentucky | 300,000 | 100,000 | | 100,000 | |
| Louisiana | 300,000 | 100,000 | | 100,000 | 300,000 |
| Maine | | | 100,000 | | 300,000 |
| Maryland | 300,000 | 100,000 | | 100,000 | |
| Massachusetts | 300,000 | 100,000 | | 100,000 | 300,000 |
| Michigan | 300,000 | 100,000 | | 100,000 | 300,000 |
| Minnesota | 300,000 | 100,000 | 100,000 | | 300,000 |
| Mississippi | 300,000 | 100,000 | | 100,000 | 300,000 |
| Missouri | 300,000 | 100,000 | | 100,000 | 300,000 |
| Montana | 300,000 | 100,000 | | 100,000 | 300,000 |
| Nebraska | 300,000 | 100,000 | | 100,000 | 300,000 |
| Nevada | 300,000 | 100,000 | | 100,000 | 300,000 |
| New Hampshire | 300,000 | 100,000 | 100,000 | 100,000 | 300,000 |
| New Jersey* | 500,000 | 100,000 | | 500,000 | 500,000 |
| New Mexico | | | 100,000 | | 300,000 |
| New York | | | | | 500,000 |
| North Carolina | | | | | 300,000 |
| North Dakota | 300,000 | 100,000 | | 100,000 | 300,000 |
| Ohio | 300,000 | 100,000 | | 100,000 | 300,000 |
| Oklahoma | 300,000 | 100,000 | | 300,000 | 300,000 |
| Oregon* | 300,000 | 100,000 | | 100,000 | 300,000 |
| Pennsylvania | 300,000 | 100,000 | 100,000 | 300,000 | 300,000 |
| Puerto Rico | 300,000 | 100,000 | | 100,000 | 300,000 |
| Rhode Island | 300,000 | 100,000 | | 100,000 | 300,000 |
| South Carolina | | | | | 300,000 |
| South Dakota | 300,000 | 100,000 | | 100,000 | 300,000 |
| Tennessee | 300,000 | 100,000 | | 100,000 | 300,000 |
| Texas | 300,000 | 100,000 | | 100,000 | |
| Utah | 300,000 | 100,000 | | 100,000 | 300,000 |
| Vermont | 300,000 | 100,000 | | 100,000 | 300,000 |
| Virginia | 300,000 | 100,000 | | 100,000 | 300,000 |
| Washington* | 500,000 | | | 500,000 | 500,000 |
| West Virginia | 300,000 | 100,000 | | 100,000 | 300,000 |
| Wisconsin | | | | | 300,000 |
| Wyoming | 300,000 | 100,000 | | 100,000 | 300,000 |

Notes: Refer to the state guaranty association acts as to what types of policies are/are not covered.

*CA There is a super-aggregate limit of $5 million per policyowner, regardless of the number of policies. There is a 20 percent deductible in the limits for life insurance and annuity policies. The limits for health insurance can increase or decrease depending on the CPI.

*NJ An annuitant cannot receive more than $100,000 in net cash values on an annuity.

*OR There is a super-aggregate limit of $5 million, subject to the limits, per any one policy or contractholder. This limit does not apply to governmental retirement plans established under Code Sections 401, 403(b) or 457.

*WA The $500,000 death benefits limit includes cash values. The $500,000 present value of annuities limit also applies to annuities established under Code Section 403(b). The $5 million unallocated annuities limit applies to unallocated annuities and governmental retirement plans established under Code Sections 401 or 457.

*Source:* National Organization of Life and Health Guaranty Associations. This chart uses information provided by NOLHGA.     5/31/96

of these risks, most annuity contracts guarantee to return 100 percent of the contractholder's principal, less any withdrawals or loans. This contractual guarantee does not eliminate the risk or the asset value fluctuation per se but assures that the contractholder's risk is limited only to the interest within the contract. This is a significant advantage the annuity has over alternative investments such as corporate or municipal bonds, as the following example shows.

Assume that in 1993, Kathy made three investments: a $100,000 short-term bond paying 7 percent interest, a $100,000 intermediate-term bond paying 7.6 percent interest and a $100,000 deferred annuity crediting 8 percent interest. If interest rates remain stable, there is no asset value fluctuation, and all three investments perform to meet Kathy's needs. But what if interest rates increase slowly by 1 percent a year for the next three years? Now, new short-term and intermediate-term bonds are yielding 10 percent and 10.6 percent, respectively, and new annuity contracts are crediting 11 percent. Kathy, who is still earning 8 percent on her annuity and is locked in to her bond rates, is no longer happy and wishes to exchange all three of her investments to get the higher interest rates.

The problem is that Kathy must get someone else to buy her 7 percent and 7.6 percent bonds when the competition within the new issue market is 3 percent higher. Obviously, there will be a price to pay for this liquidity. As Ill. 8.4 shows, Kathy will lose $5,319 of her money when she sells her short-term bond and over $16,500 on her intermediate-term bond.

This will not be the case with the annuity (unless the annuity is MVA). An annuity contract provides that the insurer absorbs the interest rate risk and guarantees that, no matter what the fluctuating value of the market may indicate, the contractholder will always get back his or her principal. Consequently, in this example, Kathy would be able to transfer the annuity values—$125,900, less any surrender charges—to another carrier, if she wants to preserve tax deferral and receive a higher rate of return on her investment. In any event, if her principal is guaranteed, her full $100,000 would be returned, regardless of surrender charges.

### ILL. 8.4 ■ *Asset Value Fluctuation*

| | Cost | Initial Rate | Value*<br>(After 3 percent increase<br>in interest rates) |
|---|---|---|---|
| Short-term bond | $100,000 | 7.0% | $94,681 |
| Intermediate-term bond | $100,000 | 7.6% | $83,442 |

*This value is the equivalent of the present value of the remaining interest plus the $100,000 principal. The short-term bond has a five-year maturity; the intermediate-term bond has a 12-year maturity.

### Insurance Companies vs. Banks and S&Ls

Many consumers look to an insurance company and want to draw immediate comparisons between insurers and other financial institutions, such as banks or savings and loans (S&Ls). These comparisons are difficult to make because banks and S&Ls have different objectives with their products and structure. Banks and S&Ls typically sell liquidity products like savings accounts, checking accounts and CDs. In addition, they have lending capabilities that make them unique and differentiate them from insurance companies. Because of these differences and the importance of their existence in our day-to-day financial life, these institutions are inexorably linked to both federal and state governments.

Banks, S&Ls and insurance companies provide certain guarantees. While banks and S&Ls enjoy the financial guarantee of the federal government, the insurance industry, in essence, puts the full faith and credit of the industry behind its contracts. Thus far, that has been sufficient to protect contractholders' principal—and without spending one penny of taxpayers' money. That same statement cannot be made by the S&L industry. In any event, banks, S&Ls and insurance companies are all considered exceedingly safe and free from most credit risk.

## ■ TAX DEFERRAL AND YIELD

> *From the standpoint of the contractholder, a deferred annuity, during its accumulation period, does not significantly differ from a long-term certificate of deposit (which, incidentally, also may be subject to penalty if it is surrendered prematurely) or any other portfolio investment which may be reduced to cash at any time. Nevertheless, interest from other portfolio investments is taxed currently whereas earnings credited to a deferred annuity are not. To the extent that annuities can be fashioned to offer interest rates that are competitive with rates paid by other financial instruments, there is little reason why a potential investor should purchase anything but a deferred annuity.*

> *—Hon. John E. Chopoton, Assistant Secretary for Tax Policy*
> *Testifying before the Senate Finance Committee*
> *March 30, 1981*

This quote goes straight to the heart of the second and third benefits annuities offer. They are:

- the ability to accumulate retirement funds on a *tax-deferred basis* and

- the ability to secure a *favorable yield* to maximize the compounding of the funds.

Because these two benefits are interrelated, we will discuss them together. The concept of tax deferral is central to the ability of the annuity to perform. The need for a competitive yield is simply a market-driven bonus that helps to improve the performance of tax deferral. To appreciate the magnitude of these benefits, we need to understand some basic terms and concepts.

### Simple Interest vs. Compound Interest

*Simple interest* is the interest that is credited on the principal. If the return on an investment is based on simple interest, then each year, the interest received will be exactly the same, as long as the interest rate is the same.

*Compound interest* is interest on interest. This means that each time interest is credited, it is credited not only on the principal amount invested, but also on the interest that has already accrued in the account. Illustration 8.5 shows the difference between simple interest and compound interest.

### Compound Interest and the Time Value of Money

Once you understand the concept of compound interest, the next step is knowing how to apply compounding over a period of time. This concept is called the *time value of money*. The combination of tax deferral, compound interest and the time value of money represents the logic behind the quote that introduced this section. To appreciate the time value of money and to understand its impact, let's consider the fate of Christopher Columbus.

---

**ILL. 8.5 ■ *Simple vs. Compound Interest***

The following table shows the difference between a $10,000 account credited with simple interest and a $10,000 account credited with annual compound interest over a 20-year period.

|  | Account A<br>$10,000 at Simple<br>7.5 Percent Interest | Account B<br>$10,000 at Compound<br>7.5 Percent Interest |
|---|---|---|
| 1 year | $10,750 | $10,750 |
| 5 years | $13,750 | $14,356 |
| 10 years | $17,500 | $20,610 |
| 15 years | $21,250 | $29,589 |
| 20 years | $25,000 | $42,479 |

In 1492, Christopher Columbus sailed across the great Atlantic Ocean and came upon the new world. A little known fact at the time was the existence of two financial institutions, the Old World Bank and the New World Bank. Intrigued, Columbus decided that he wanted to start his retirement program in America.

Columbus walked into the New World Bank and put down his only asset at the time, a bottle of Italian Pinot Grigio. The clerk explained that in America wine could not be used as an asset to be deposited into a retirement plan, but he offered the navigator $2 for the bottle. Being somewhat cautious, Columbus took the $2 and deposited one dollar into the New World Bank's SuperThen passbook account, paying 5 percent compound interest.

Happy with his investment, Columbus headed down the street looking for the nearest video store. Before reaching his destination, he walked by the Old World Bank, which touted a marquee offering a 10 percent simple interest passbook account. Furious at the thought of missing an opportunity to get twice as much interest, but too tired to return to the New World Bank and get his money back, Columbus decided to open a second account with the Old World Bank using his remaining dollar. Little did Columbus know how smart he was. It turns out that the banks only had NWDIC (New World Deposit Insurance Corporation) insurance protection good up to $1 per institution.

Back to Spain went our Italian friend where he eventually died. Five hundred years following his death, his estate cleared probate, and the last two remaining descendants of the Columbus bloodline came to America to collect their riches. Into the Old World Bank walked the first of the descendants. Upon presentation of the 500-year-old parchbook, the first descendant received a check for $51.

You see, simple interest is simple because it's easy. The 10 percent simple interest amounted to one dime a year for 500 years, or $50; in addition, there is the return of the original $1 investment. Obviously, this investment left something to be desired.

Not familiar with the concept of compound interest and the time value of money, the other Columbus descendant feared that there would only be $26 in the New World Bank account, because the interest rate was half that of the Old World Bank. That fear quickly subsided when the president of the bank came out to present the heir with a check for $39,323,261,830, the result of $1 compounded for 500 years at 5 percent compound interest. Such is the value of compound interest and the time value of money.

## Add Tax Deferral

When you add the concept of tax deferral, the numbers can be overwhelming. Let's consider a more reasonable example of how tax deferral, compounding and the time value of money can be utilized to educate a prospective client as to the benefits of the annuity.

## ILL. 8.6 ■ *Annuities vs. Alternative Investments*

**A**ssume an individual has $100,000 to invest and is considering three investment alternatives. He or she is a 40 percent (combined state and federal) taxpayer. The following shows how tax deferral gives the annuity a significant advantage over the other two investments.*

|  | Certificate of Deposit | Money Market Fund | Annuity |
|---|---|---|---|
| Before-tax yield: | 6.50% | 6.10% | 7.75% |
| After-tax yield: | 3.90% | 3.66% | 7.75% |
| 1 year | $103,900 | $103,660 | $107,750 |
| 5 years | $121,081 | $119,689 | $145,240 |
| 10 years | $146,607 | $143,255 | $210,947 |
| 15 years | $177,514 | $171,461 | $306,379 |
| 20 years | $214,937 | $205,221 | $444,985 |

*All three investments assume the same rate of return over 20 years and annual compounding. After 20 years, the annuity value after taxes is $306,991.

Assume Carl, age 45, has $100,000 and is considering three investments: a one-year CD, a money market fund and a deferred annuity. As shown in Ill. 8.6, the before-tax yields on these investments are 6.5 percent, 6.1 percent and 7.75 percent, respectively. However, Carl must pay current income taxes on the CD and money market fund returns. Consequently, because Carl is a 40 percent taxpayer, the net yields on the investments drop to 3.90 percent and 3.66 percent, respectively. But the yield on the annuity, because of tax deferral, remains at 7.75 percent.

The difference between these investment options becomes very apparent when you review the 10-year and 20-year figures, which show how compounding, tax deferral and the time value of money put the annuity far ahead of the alternatives.

Even assuming a "worst case" scenario, the annuity still outperforms the other two investments. The "worst case" would be where Carl enjoys tax deferral for 20 years and then decides to liquidate his annuity for a lump-sum payout, without taking advantage of any of the distribution options we've learned about. A lump-sum payout means that Carl would have to pay taxes on the annuity's interest earnings, which would amount to $137,994. Yet, even with the tax Carl would still have almost $307,000. By comparison, the CD—the nearest alternative—is almost $92,000 less in value.

## Taxable Equivalent Yields

To be effective in selling the concept of the annuity's tax deferral, you must be able to calculate and explain the significance of *taxable equivalent yields*. A taxable equivalent yield is what a taxable investment must yield to make that investment equal to a tax-deferred investment. For example, let's say that the current yield on an annuity is 8 percent. For an individual in a 31 percent tax bracket, the taxable equivalent yield necessary to equal the annuity yield would be 11.59 percent. In other words, that individual would need to find a comparable taxable investment yielding 11.59 percent to equal a tax-deferred annuity yield of 8 percent. Illustration 8.7 contains a sample chart of tax-deferred yields and their corresponding tax equivalent yields, as well as simple formulas for calculating the tax-deferred and taxable equivalent yields.

---

### ILL. 8.7 ■ *Taxable Equivalent Yields*

The following table shows the yields necessary on taxable investments to accumulate the same amount of money as a tax-deferred annuity, per income tax bracket.

|  | 15% Tax Bracket | 28% Tax Bracket | 31% Tax Bracket |
|---|---|---|---|
| Tax-deferred yield: | 6.00%  7.00%  8.00% | 6.00%  7.00%  8.00% | 6.00%  7.00%  8.00% |
| Taxable equivalent yield: | 7.06%  8.24%  9.41% | 8.33%  9.72%  11.11% | 8.70%  10.14%  11.59% |

It's fairly easy to calculate either the taxable equivalent yield or the tax-deferred yield. If you know one, you can determine the other. The formula for the taxable equivalent yield is:

*Tax deferred yield ÷ (100% − the tax bracket)*

Example: The investor is a 15 percent taxpayer and the tax-deferred yield on an annuity is 7.05 percent. The equivalent yield he or she would have to find on a taxable investment would be 8.3 percent:

*.0705 ÷ (1.00 − .15) = .083 = 8.3 percent*

If you want to know the equivalent *tax-deferred yield* of a taxable yield, the formula is:

*(100% − the tax bracket) × the taxable yield*

Example: For an individual in the 28 percent tax bracket who has a taxable investment yielding 8 percent, an annuity yielding only 5.8 percent would generate the same amount of money:

*(1.00 − .28) × .08 = .058 = 5.8 percent*

## ■ LIQUIDITY

*Liquidity* is the next annuity benefit and one that cannot be overstated. The means by which a contractholder can access the values in his or her annuity have been discussed in previous chapters, but they are worth reviewing briefly.

### Free Withdrawals

Most annuity contracts provide liquidity through *free withdrawals*. As we discussed, the free withdrawal provision can be expressed as the annual accumulated interest within the contract, as a percentage of the accumulated account value or as a percentage of the premium deposits. Free withdrawal privileges are typically not cumulative. In other words, if the privilege is not used in any given contract year, the unused benefit may not be added to the next contract year's benefit.

### Loans

Annuity *loans* are another means of liquidity. Though loan provisions are most typically found in qualified tax-sheltered annuities, some of the new nonqualified annuities designed over the past few years have also incorporated loan provisions. These loans are typically available to the contractholder at a low net cost. However, annuity loans are considered a distribution from the contract and therefore are taxable. If the loan is taken before the age of 59½, a 10 percent early withdrawal penalty will also apply.

### Nursing Home/Hospitalization Provision

Another form of liquidity found in most fixed and variable annuities today is a *waiver of surrender charge* if the contractholder is confined to a licensed nursing facility or undergoes a long period of hospitalization. However, for the practitioner selling annuities that provide these waivers, a note of caution is in order. Because the insurance company must protect itself against antiselection, the application may ask if the applicant has been or is about to be confined to a hospital or licensed nursing facility. If the applicant answers that question affirmatively, the contract may not be issued.

### Full Surrender

The most obvious form of liquidity within the annuity contract is the *full surrender.* As long as the contract does not specifically preclude surrender, the contractholder can always surrender the contract for the surrender value. The surrender value is most typically expressed as premium deposits plus interest minus free withdrawals minus surrender charges. The surrender value is almost always guaranteed not to invade principal.

Some of the new annuity products being marketed today contain provisions that allow the contractholder, if diagnosed as terminally ill, to withdraw part or all of his or her account balance, free of surrender charges. In addition, a select few contracts give contractholders access to their accumulated account value in the event they lose their jobs. The practitioner should review such provisions very carefully to determine if there are any definitional restrictions and to understand how broadly or narrowly these provisions may apply.

## ■ PROBATE AVOIDANCE

*Probate* is the process that the state uses to identify assets within a decedent's estate for purposes of determining tax liability, executing the will and distributing property to beneficiaries and heirs. If no will exists, the probate process provides for the orderly payment of claims from the estate and disposal of the assets of the estate. The process of probating an estate can entail three drawbacks—publicity, delay and expense—none of which an annuity is subject to.

### Publicity

The probate process requires that, upon the death of an estate owner, notice be given to all interested parties—such as relatives and creditors—so that they may bring forth their claims against the estate. Though most states allow notification through either letter or publication, most estates are publicly probated by publishing a notice in local newspapers.

### Delay

The minimum delay in probating an estate is six months from the date of the last notice. As such, the probate process can take years, as creditors and others with an interest in the decedent's estate are offered an opportunity to stake their claim to the assets of the estate. This means that heirs and beneficiaries of the estate property subject to probate must wait until the process is complete before they receive their bequests.

### Expense

Finally, the cost of the probate process can be exorbitant. All assets within the probated estate are subject to fees. Typically, those fees are assessed by attorneys or executors who usually charge a percentage of the probated estate for their services. In addition, there may be costs for conservators and appraisers as well as other costs deemed appropriate by the probate court.

Annuities avoid all of these problems because the annuity is a contract issued by a life insurance company. As such, its proceeds pass directly and immediately to the named beneficiary by virtue of the provisions of the contract, and not through the process of probate.

## ■ ANNUITY FEES

The annuity is typically sold as a back-end loaded contract. As such, no fees are deducted at the time of the product's purchase. If the contractholder purchases a flexible premium annuity, there may be some annual fee for the administration of these small premium amounts.

Some might argue that surrender charges can be considered fees. However, surrender charges in an annuity contract are usually limited in their duration and almost always guarantee not to invade principal. This is significantly different from other investments, such as a CD that has a revolving surrender charge or a bond that has asset value fluctuation.

## ■ SUMMARY

In this chapter, we examined the many benefits of today's deferred annuities. We looked at the increasingly important issue of insurance company solvency, and what state regulators have done to improve the safety of this already conservative industry and its annuity products. We have also looked at the other consumer benefits of the annuity to gain a better appreciation of what the annuity product has to offer in comparison with other types of investments. We're now ready to apply those benefits to the markets for annuities.

## ■ CHAPTER 8 QUESTIONS FOR REVIEW

1.  All of the following are risks specifically evaluated by the risk-based capital method, EXCEPT:

    a. asset risk.
    b. mortality risk.
    c. business risk.
    d. systems risk.

2.  Most fixed annuities do NOT mitigate the effect of asset value fluctuation.

    *True* or *False*

3. The state insurance commissioners regulate separately, but together they form an association called the

   a. NASD.
   b. SEC.
   c. NALU.
   d. NAIC.

4. Which rating agency utilizes both claims-paying ability and qualified solvency ratings?

   a. Standard & Poor's
   b. Duff & Phelps
   c. A.M. Best
   d. Moody's

5. All of the following affect the time value "compounding" of money, EXCEPT:

   a. length of compound period.
   b. interest rate credited.
   c. method of compounding.
   d. quality of investment.

# 9

## Annuity Markets and Uses

I n this chapter, we will answer the questions of who the annuity buyer is and why people buy annuities. We will cover the demographics and psycho-graphics of the markets as they exist today and show how to measure their applicability in your marketing efforts. In addition, we will review the many uses of the annuity and how it solves problems for those who purchase them.

■ ■ ■ ■ ■

### ■ IDENTIFYING THE ANNUITY BUYER

Who is the annuity buyer? A survey conducted by the Life Insurance Marketing and Research Association (LIMRA) suggests that two-thirds of annuity contracts are pur-chased by individuals 45 years old or older and the average annuity purchase is around $25,000. While these statistics will differ from company to company, they give us a general picture of the typical annuity buyer. However, for practitioners to maximize their effectiveness in marketing annuities, they must be able to:

- differentiate between market segments and

- capitalize on the potential of this market by breaking it down into perceptible buying units.

In this chapter, we will look at a number of ways that the annuity market can be divided and prospective buyers identified. This procedure is known as "market segmentation."

## ■ MARKET SEGMENTATION

*Market segmentation* is the process of distinguishing groups of buyers or prospects according to certain variables or characteristics they have in common. Prospects differ in one or more ways. For example, they may differ in their needs, desires, ages, income brackets or buying attitudes. They may differ in their philosophy on investments or savings or in their tolerance to financial risk. Any of these variables can be used to segment a market. One of the results of market segmentation is the identification of prospect needs, preferences and motivators, which allows the practitioner to develop a proper approach and make a proper product recommendation.

Actually, market segmentation is something that we do instinctively in sales. For example, we don't try to sell a fixed annuity to someone who has just graduated from college and has no money. However, over the past decade or so, our information processing systems, communication systems and research analysis techniques have improved so much that instincts can be enhanced through the use of segmentation techniques.

### Demographic Segmentation

*Demographics* are quantifiable statistics. "How old are you?" "Where do you live?" "How much do you make?" These are all examples of demographic information. In essence, they are indisputable statements of fact. You would use demographic research, for example, to ascertain a city, suburb or neighborhood of high-wage earners and then conduct annuity prospecting in those areas.

### Psychographic Segmentation

*Pyschographics* survey harder-to-quantify intangibles. Psychographics segment markets or buyers on the basis of values or lifestyles or attitudes. "Why did you buy that product?" "How do you feel about where you live?" "What are your fears as they relate to investments?" These questions are all examples of how one would collect psychographic information. Just like demographic information, psychographic information can be invaluable when positioning your marketing efforts. Psychographics can be used to help quantify risk tolerance, an integral element in identifying annuity buyers.

### Age Segmentation

Age is a key factor in understanding the annuity market. *Age segmentation* allows you to match effectively the prospect's needs and objectives with the various annuity product designs and benefits. For example, the older the prospect, the more likely he or she is to buy the single-premium fixed annuity. The younger the prospect, the more likely the sale will be oriented toward the flexible premium annuity, and perhaps the variable design instead of the fixed. The greater the need for income, a likely

## ILL. 9.1 ■ *Demographics vs. Psychographics*

Segmenting a market based on demographics and psychographics is a popular and effective way to prospect for annuity business. Because individual wants and needs change with age and vary according to income, demographic segmentation calls for dividing the market based on quantifiable demographic information such as age or income. Psychographics segment the market according to lifestyles, values or attitudes. Individuals within the same demographic group can display very different psychographic traits.

| Demographics | Psychographics |
|---|---|
| "Where do you live?" | "What is your political affiliation?" |
| "How much do you make?" | "What are your attitudes toward risk?" |
| "How many children do you have?" | "Why do you buy something?" |
| "What is your age?" | "What are your fears/concerns?" |
| "What is your occupation?" | "What makes you laugh or cry?" |

possibility with older prospects at retirement, the more the annuity's distribution options will look attractive.

The average age of the (nonqualified) single-premium fixed annuity buyer is approximately 58, and the average premium deposited is around $33,000. From the standpoint of psychographics, the fixed annuity buyer tends to be motivated by safety, liquidity and tax deferral.

It is typical in the fixed annuity sale for the older prospect to look for guarantees. For example, guarantees of interest rate, costs, benefit payouts and the like would be very important to this type of buyer. For these individuals, the bailout annuity or the certificate annuity should go a long way toward meeting their needs.

From a psychographic viewpoint, individuals experience different emotional problems and needs as they grow older. A prospect who is in his or her mid-50s will be more concerned with tax deferral and inflation protection. A prospect who is 68 years old will share the inflation concern but could be more interested in safety and income than tax deferral.

The variable annuity adds yet another dimension to the annuity product line, based on its appeal to the younger or less risk-adverse audience. The average age of the variable annuity buyer is about 46, and the average premium deposited is around $22,000. This reflects the obvious differences between the two markets. Younger individuals are more likely to take some risk in their investments. Also, because younger people have had less time to accumulate assets and theoretically are earning less, the average amount deposited in a variable annuity is somewhat less than in the fixed annuity.

## Geo-demographic Segmentation

There will always be exceptions to these age segments. There is a new market analysis technique called *geo-demographics* that attempts to incorporate geographic information with demographic data in order to further segment a market. This type of segmentation can create variations in your marketing.

Let's say that your town has only two suburbs. Both of the suburbs are old and established and enjoy a wealthy population base. One suburb is known as a place to which young entrepreneurs are gravitating. The other is also attracting young people, but they are of a more conservative following, with lower risk tolerance.

Geo-demographic segmentation would reveal that the more conservative suburb will be more responsive to the fixed annuity, whereas the inhabitants of the first suburb are more likely to mix their investments between the fixed and variable annuity. By looking at geo-demographic information, we can combine demographics and psychographics and adjust for geographic realities.

## Income/Asset Segmentation

Another segmentation method that can be used is *income/asset segmentation*. Theoretically speaking, income and assets should be key attributes in quantifying the annuity market. The more income or assets an individual has, the greater the tax burden and the more appealing the annuity will be. An individual earning $200,000 a year as a corporate executive would probably not have a need for income but would certainly be interested in tax deferral. On the other hand, someone earning $25,000 a year may not be primarily motivated by tax deferral but could be attracted to the annuity as a way to accumulate retirement funds.

## Product Segmentation

*Product segmentation* provides the opportunity to segment a market by similar product characteristics. For example, let's say that you only want to sell single-premium fixed annuities. Your research indicates that the appeal of the fixed annuity is somewhat similar to the CD, as far as its benefits to potential buyers. Product segmentation would suggest that you buy a list of CD owners and prospect among those individuals for single-premium fixed annuity business.

## ■ USING SEGMENTATION

You can segment any market you wish in any number of ways. If you thought that people who wore blue suits were more likely to purchase annuities, you could segment accordingly. However, not all segmentations are valid. The keys to good segmentation are first, a proper understanding of the demographics and psychographics of the marketplace—what variables are relevant to the purchase of annuities—and second, a focused approach to marketing. The key characteristics of market segments are noted in Ill. 9.2.

You need to look at segmentation as a multifaceted tool. For instance, segmentation for age should also be accompanied by segmentation for income; otherwise, your focus will be diluted. Let's say you have identified the fixed annuity market as a primary market. By nature of your product decision, you must segment by age *and* income. If you only segment by income or assets, the result would be a field too broad to consider. The same thing would occur if you only segment by age. You could qualify a lot of potential prospects by age, but they may or may not have the adequate resources to invest in an annuity.

Let's look at how a "multi-attribute" approach to segmentation, using age as the base segment, can point to different profiles of the annuity buyer. Each profile calls for a distinct marketing or sales approach.

---

### ILL. 9.2 ■ *Characteristics of Useful Market Segments*

**M**arkets can be segmented in many ways. For example, you could identify annuity buyers according to the kinds of cars they drive. However, it's unlikely that this variable is pertinent to the purchase of annuities. To be useful, market segments should have the following characteristics:

- *Measurable*. A good market segment should be measurable by size and its potential purchasing power.

- *Accessible*. A good market segment should be one that you can effectively reach, approach and serve.

- *Large enough to sustain your marketing efforts*. A good market segment should contain enough homogeneous prospects to make a concerted, focused marketing effort worthwhile.

- *Workable*. A good market segment should point to a specific marketing approach or plan, making use of the characteristics its members have in common.

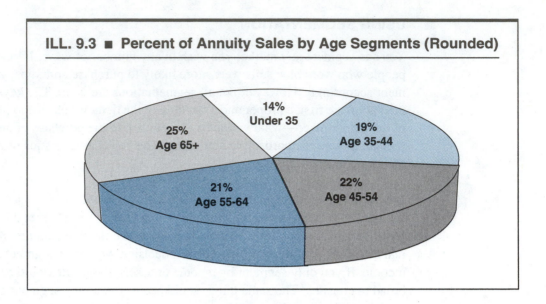

### ILL. 9.3 ■ Percent of Annuity Sales by Age Segments (Rounded)

## Understanding the Annuity Buyer—Age Segmentation

There are three primary age segments that comprise the annuity market: 45 to 55, 56 to 65 and over 65. By understanding the differences that exist among these segments, the practitioner can begin to develop a marketing strategy that maximizes segmentation techniques.

### Ages 45 to 55

The 45-year-old to 55-year-old market is characterized by individuals who are entering, or are in, the prime of their income-earning years. These individuals are interested in tax deferral and future benefits. Because this segment of the market is subject to the pre-age 59½ penalty for early withdrawals, the nature of the annuity becomes long-term tax deferral. This segment of the market is also likely to be willing to take some risk with their investments, suggesting that the separate account options of the variable annuity might have appeal. Finally, because many of the individuals who are at the lower ages of this market may not yet have accumulated large sums of money, the flexible premium annuity may be very appealing.

### Ages 56 to 65

The 56-year-old to 65-year-old market segment is a diverse cross-section of the market. Generally, these people are also motivated by deferral and future benefits. However, some members of this segment may need benefits today, which points to the annuity's distribution options and advantages.

When selling in this market, the annuity's flexibility should be stressed. In addition, safety becomes a primary concern, much more so than at the younger ages. In this market, the practitioner will be competing with CDs and other time deposits that are sold on the basis of safety and liquidity. As such, the practitioner should point out the annuity provides safety, liquidity *and* tax deferral.

> ### ILL. 9.4 ■ *Differentiating Annuities and CDs*
>
> In the past, many comparisons have been made between certificates of deposit (CDs) and annuities. Some of these comparisons are fair and accurate; some are not. Let's try to set the record straight.
>
> A CD is a time deposit insured by the FDIC guarantee that protects such bank assets with a limit of $1 million. Certificates of deposit should be viewed as short-term investments in that their yields are based on short-term assets. While maturities typically extend out to five years, most CD customers elect one-year or three-year time horizons. The earnings on CDs are taxable unless the product is held in a qualified account. Finally, CDs carry a loss-of-interest penalty that extends for the full term of the contract if it is cashed in before it matures.
>
> An annuity is not a short-term investment. It rewards the buyer who commits to tax deferral and that reward is more dramatic every year. The annuity is not guaranteed by the FDIC, but there is no limit in terms of protection by the insurance company. The annuity has a finite period during which surrender charges apply. Unlike CDs, annuity monies are invested by the insurer for 6 to 10 years, depending on the terms of the contract. The annuity offers liquidity in addition to tax deferral through free withdrawals, loans and surrender charge waivers under certain circumstances. Finally, whereas the value of a CD could be part of the owner's estate at death, the annuity passes outside of probate to the named beneficiary.

Interestingly, liquidity can be a prime motivator in this market, but it is typically not well presented in the sale of an annuity. Consider Ill. 9.6, which compares the liquidity of the CD with that of the annuity. In this example, the CD is a one-year CD, with a six-month loss of interest penalty. There is a seven-day window at the end of each year during which the owner can access the CD values without a penalty. Contrast that to the annuity, which has a six-year surrender charge period and a 10 percent free withdrawal option. In terms of liquidity, what do these two options offer over a 10-year period?

With the CD, the owner has a total of 70 days of liquidity, either partial or total. All 70 of these days fall at the same time of year, when the CD matures. In other words, if the investor is not able to plan his or her emergency cash needs to coincide with the renewal of the CD, there will be a penalty.

By contrast, the annuity provides a 10 percent free withdrawal option, which can be utilized at any time during each of the first six years, followed by complete freedom to withdraw without penalty after six years. Which product provides more liquidity? Which product provides tax deferral as well?

One final note on the age 56 to 65 market: This market tends to gravitate toward the fixed annuity and generally purchases the annuity with a single premium.

## ILL. 9.5 ■ *Fixed vs. Variable Annuities: Who Buys What?*

| Age Segment | Percentage Who Buy Fixed Annuities | Percentage Who Buy Variable Annuities |
|---|---|---|
| 70 and over | 83% | 17% |
| 60–69 | 73% | 27% |
| 50–59 | 55% | 45% |
| 40–49 | 36% | 64% |
| 30–39 | 32% | 68% |
| 20–29 | 32% | 68% |
| Under 20 | 67% | 33% |

### Over 65

In the over-65 market, there are three primary reasons why individuals buy annuities: safety, safety and safety. Other benefits annuities hold for this market include income distribution and guarantees, flexible liquidity options, probate avoidance and for some, tax deferral. Because preservation of principal is very important to these individuals, the focus of an annuity presentation should remain on safety, including the benefit of avoiding asset value fluctuation.

Age segmentation is only the first step in developing an annuity market. As the annuity market overall continues to grow, and as the industry becomes more and more aware of the communication and research capabilities that exist, segmentation will become one of the most important tools in the annuity sale.

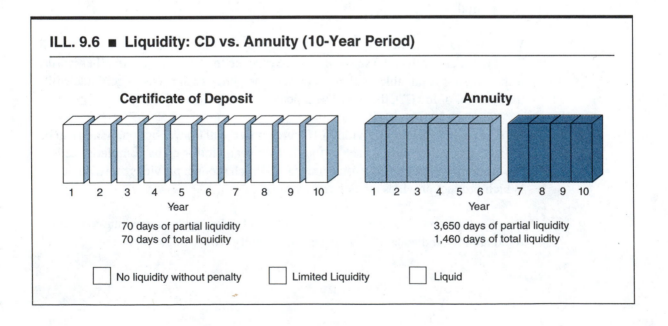

## ILL. 9.6 ■ Liquidity: CD vs. Annuity (10-Year Period)

**Certificate of Deposit**

1 2 3 4 5 6 7 8 9 10
Year

70 days of partial liquidity
70 days of total liquidity

**Annuity**

1 2 3 4 5 6 7 8 9 10
Year

3,650 days of partial liquidity
1,460 days of total liquidity

☐ No liquidity without penalty    ☐ Limited Liquidity    ☐ Liquid

## ■ WHY DO PEOPLE BUY ANNUITIES?

In Chapter 8 we discussed the basic benefits that the annuity offers. In this chapter we will look at how those benefits apply to the consumer and how the annuity solves problems for the consumer. Keep in mind that as a financial advisor, you are not paid to sell products but to solve problems. Let's see how the annuity can solve your clients' problems.

### The Tax Problem

A problem that many people face, and one that has been mentioned many times throughout this text, is the problem of deferring taxation on funds that are earmarked for retirement. How does this problem manifest itself to the client? One way is through the yearly payment of taxes and filing of Form 1040 with Uncle Sam. So, how can the annuity solve the problem of paying too much in taxes, and how can you illustrate that problem and solution to your prospect?

Illustration 9.7 shows a portion of a prospect's 1040 tax form. As you can see, the prospect declared $12,000 in interest income from his bank and savings and loan. As a 31 percent taxpayer, this individual will pay over $3,700 in taxes this year on these investments alone. The reason that this individual had over $3,700 in taxes is that he currently has $150,000 in taxable CDs and savings accounts earning 8 percent.

Once you have identified this problem, you can suggest that the prospect reposition an inefficient asset—notably, two-thirds of the $150,000—and purchase an annuity. The next time this individual files his Form 1040, all things being equal, he will declare only $4,000 in interest. This will result in a tax of approximately $1,200 instead of $3,700. Simply by repositioning some assets, you have helped save $2,500 in taxes for this individual. Furthermore, because annuities generally credit a higher interest rate than passbook savings, CDs or money market funds, you may have also rewarded this person with a higher yield.

### Diversification

Many people have limited resources. They cannot diversify their investments because of these limited resources. Consequently, these individuals may be naturally inclined to buy a mutual fund, thereby gaining the diversification that they cannot achieve on their own. However, many of these same people do not wish to be subject to asset value fluctuation and the impact that outside factors such as interest rates may have on their investment.

Both fixed and variable annuities can either partially or entirely eliminate asset value fluctuation. The fixed annuity almost always eliminates asset value fluctuation, unless there is a market value adjustment. In those cases, fluctuation is only partially eliminated. Depending on its design, the variable annuity may offer some protection against asset value fluctuation. The bottom line is that the annuity will provide

## ILL. 9.7 ■ Repositioning Assets to Save Taxes

### Before Repositioning

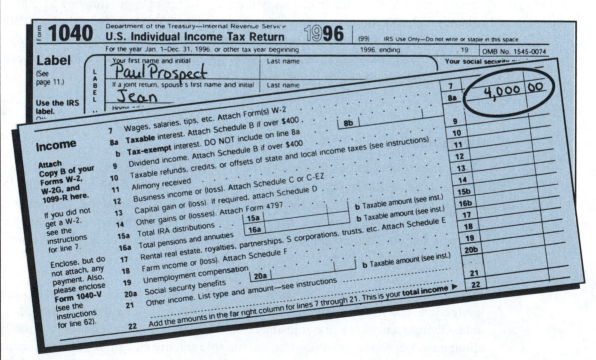

### After Repositioning

diversification for the investor and will mitigate the negative effect of asset value fluctuation.

### Income

The annuity can also be used to provide income. For this purpose, the contractholder has the option to take systematic withdrawals or annuitize the contract. Either option provides guarantees that are not available with other income vehicles, such as bonds. In addition, the annuity has certain other benefits. For example, if a contractholder were to take withdrawals from his or her annuity systematically, as opposed to annuitizing, the deferred element of the annuity would continue to enjoy tax deferral and the chance for asset value appreciation. If interest rates increase in the market, the annuity, unlike a bond, should gradually reflect those changes through incremental increases in the credited interest rate. The bond interest rate will not change. To take advantage of the higher interest rates in the market, the bondholder would have to sell the old bond and buy a new one, resulting in fees and asset value fluctuation.

### Yield

When the deferred annuity was enjoying its first wave of popularity, the primary focus was on yield and safety. As a matter of fact, yield has been both the hero and villain in annuity sales. During the early 1980s and through the end of the decade, yield was the basis for competition in the annuity market. Eventually, the competition to offer high yields forced insurers to compromise the quality of their investment portfolios. Following the financial backlash over losses associated with aggressive investing, the industry returned to a more sensible approach to investing and crediting interest rates on annuities.

Because of the significant advantages of tax deferral, annuity yields only have to be as competitive as the A or AA quality of the investment portfolios that support these products. From a marketing standpoint, the burden falls on other investments to offer a yield that equals the annuity, after accounting for the taxes that must be paid on the alternative investments. Beyond that, other features—like indexing renewal rates to a market index—can ensure that the yield on the annuity will be fair to the contractholder and provide some degree of inflation protection. The practitioner should put yield into perspective when making annuity presentations.

## ■ THE QUALIFIED ANNUITY MARKET

Annuities hold a special place in qualified plans and can serve as excellent funding vehicles. However, as most practitioners who work the qualified market have experienced, the argument always becomes, "Why use a tax-sheltered product when you already have tax sheltering by virtue of the qualification of the plan with the IRS?" The answer can be summed up as follows: safety, yield and asset value protection.

## Safety

As we have stressed throughout this text, the insurance industry goes to great lengths to provide safety and security for its contractholders and their investments. When the issue is qualified pension plans and IRAs, employers and individuals are rightfully cautious about the way they invest those monies. Accordingly, the size, profitability and track record of the insurance industry provides a natural attraction to those interested in protecting their retirement funds.

## Yield

The yield that a qualified annuity receives is likely to be equivalent to the yield on a high-quality, moderate-duration bond fund. In addition, the annuity is backed by the safety of the industry and the guarantees it promises. Moreover, it is the insurance company that worries about the reinvestment risk, interest rate risk and credit risk, leaving the contractholder with a secure, high-yielding retirement plan.

## Asset Value Protection

The final reason to consider at least the fixed annuity to fund a qualified retirement plan is the protection the contractholder will get in relation to asset value fluctuation. With the exception of low-yielding money market funds and CDs, most other investment options would place a prospect's or client's retirement funds at risk relative to asset value fluctuation. It bears repeating that the insurance company—not the contractholder—absorbs the risk of fluctuating assets and guarantees that the contractholder's principal will always be intact.

## Where to Find Qualified Money

In the qualified market, the most common opportunities for sales professionals are IRAs and TSAs. These two retirement alternatives are directly controlled by the individual, and annuities are commonly used as a funding vehicle for these plans.

Though the complexities of qualified retirement markets are beyond the scope of this text, there are some basic differences between IRAs and TSAs that merit discussion.

### IRAs

In comparison to TSAs, IRAs are more common because they are available to more people and there are fewer restrictions on where and how IRA money can be invested.

Over the years, there have been a number of changes to the rules that govern the deductibility of IRA contributions. Currently, individuals who are not eligible to participate in a qualified employer-sponsored plan may contribute up to $2,000 of earned income to an IRA each year and deduct the full amount. Married couples who are not covered by an employer plan can contribute and deduct up to $4,000 a year to an IRA.

The rules change for those who are eligible to participate in a qualified employer plan. Though they are still allowed to contribute to an IRA, their tax deduction may be limited. The limit depends on the amount of their AGI and filing status. For example, single filers who are covered by an employer plan and whose AGI is $25,000 or less may take up to the full $2,000 maximum deduction. As AGI exceeds $25,000, the amount of the allowable IRA deduction is phased down gradually. Deductibility is lost completely when AGI reaches $35,000. For married individuals filing jointly, when either or both are covered by an employer plan, the full deduction is available if AGI is less than $40,000. Again, this deduction is phased down gradually as AGI rises. Once joint AGI reaches $50,000, no deduction for IRA contributions is allowed.

The restrictions on deducting IRA contributions have had a somewhat negative effect on the popularity of these plans; however, the fact remains that most people can still make contributions to an IRA and have those funds accumulate, tax deferred, for retirement. Consequently, the IRA market is a strong one for the sale of annuities, notably flexible premium annuities.

Today, almost half of all IRA assets are invested with banks. From this statistic, it is obvious that safety and preservation of principal is a primary objective for IRA owners. Because the annuity does not compromise safety and it typically credits higher interest rates than investments offered by banks, the annuity IRA offers the consumer a viable alternative.

### TSAs

As noted previously, tax-sheltered annuities are subject to a number of restrictions as to how and where their funds can be invested. These restrictions are more a function of the trustees of TSA plans than they are government mandates. Most TSA trustees, whether overseeing a plan for public education employees or one for 501(c)(3) employees, limit the investment alternatives that the participants have to choose from. As this relates to annuities, the trustees may allow only one or two insurers to provide products to the plan participants.

Because the insurer selection process can be political, the practitioner should be cautious and realistic when entering this market. On the other hand, an enormous opportunity exists with the TSA rollover market—rolling over TSA account balances from one product into another. A rollover might take place, for example, when a TSA participant wants certain features found in one annuity that are not available in another. Whereas trustees tend to mandate acceptable insurers for TSA plans, most allow a rollover to an insurer not formally approved by the trustee.

The TSA market also presents an excellent opportunity for follow-up sales of nonqualified annuities. Individuals in a TSA plan have a greater appreciation of the annuity than those who have not invested in the product.

## ■ BALANCE SHEET POSITIONING

As noted in an earlier chapter, practitioners typically approach the sale of life insurance from the perspective of the prospect's cash flow. In other words, they determine how much premium the prospect's income can afford. An annuity is not sold this way. The annuity is a *balance sheet sale*, and must be positioned in this manner if the practitioner is to be successful in marketing and selling these products.

A "balance sheet sale" involves analyzing a prospect's assets and liabilities and seeks to reposition or redirect any inefficient assets. The balance sheet is the perfect tool to use to identify any such assets. Illustration 9.8 is a sample balance sheet that holds many annuity sales possibilities. The first place to look is at the prospect's cash and cash equivalents. Here we see an individual with almost $123,000 in cash and cash equivalents. This money is being taxed each and every year, unless the individual is utilizing tax-free money market accounts. Allowing that this person should maintain

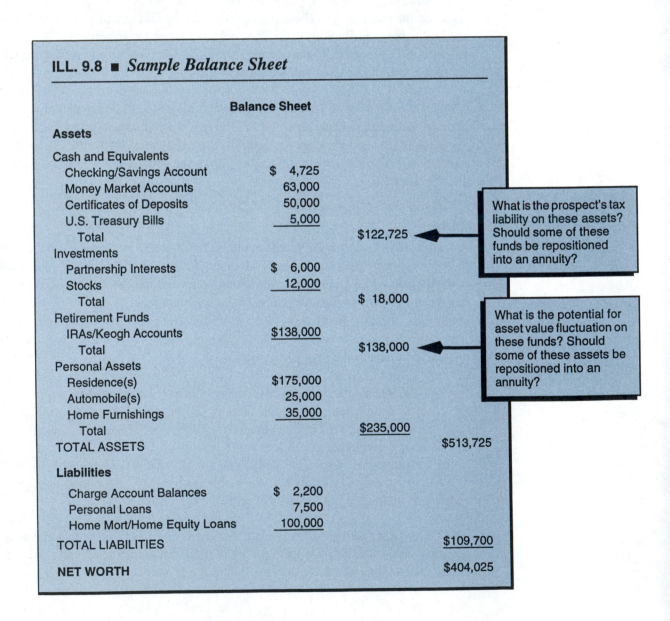

**ILL. 9.8** ■ *Sample Balance Sheet*

**Balance Sheet**

**Assets**

Cash and Equivalents
| | | |
|---|---|---|
| Checking/Savings Account | $ 4,725 | |
| Money Market Accounts | 63,000 | |
| Certificates of Deposits | 50,000 | |
| U.S. Treasury Bills | 5,000 | |
| Total | | $122,725 |

*What is the prospect's tax liability on these assets? Should some of these funds be repositioned into an annuity?*

Investments
| | | |
|---|---|---|
| Partnership Interests | $ 6,000 | |
| Stocks | 12,000 | |
| Total | | $ 18,000 |

Retirement Funds
| | | |
|---|---|---|
| IRAs/Keogh Accounts | $138,000 | |
| Total | | $138,000 |

*What is the potential for asset value fluctuation on these funds? Should some of these assets be repositioned into an annuity?*

Personal Assets
| | | |
|---|---|---|
| Residence(s) | $175,000 | |
| Automobile(s) | 25,000 | |
| Home Furnishings | 35,000 | |
| Total | | $235,000 |
| TOTAL ASSETS | | $513,725 |

**Liabilities**

| | | |
|---|---|---|
| Charge Account Balances | $ 2,200 | |
| Personal Loans | 7,500 | |
| Home Mort/Home Equity Loans | 100,000 | |
| TOTAL LIABILITIES | | $109,700 |

| | |
|---|---|
| **NET WORTH** | $404,025 |

a reasonable emergency fund or other short-term savings, he or she should certainly consider an annuity. Simply by calculating how much this prospect is paying in taxes on his or her cash and cash equivalents, the practitioner should be able to reposition some of these assets into an annuity.

In addition to cash and cash equivalents, the practitioner should look at the prospect's invested assets and examine the potential for, and the prospect's tolerance of, asset value fluctuation. In our sample case, these assets would include the individual's vested Keogh benefits and IRAs, which total $138,000—potentially more assets that should be repositioned. Using the balance sheet is the only proper way to position the annuity sale.

## ■ AVOIDING THE SOCIAL SECURITY BENEFIT TAX

Annuities can also be used by retirees to avoid or reduce the Social Security benefit tax. For individuals who are receiving Social Security benefits, the IRS has made life more complicated. If these individuals (and their spouses) have income in excess of certain levels, Social Security benefits become taxable. In this context, "income" means wages, pension benefits, investment and interest earnings (taxable and tax free) and Social Security payments. The formula used to determine the taxation of Social Security benefits can result in up to 85 percent of those benefits being taxed.

The formula differentiates between single and married taxpayers and applies two step-rate thresholds to the taxpayer's adjusted gross income. For single filers, the thresholds are set at $25,000 and $34,000; for married couples, the thresholds are $32,000 and $44,000. To the extent that income exceeds these thresholds, some amount of the taxpayer's Social Security benefit is taxable. The amount subject to taxation is the lesser of a three-part comparison. (The formula for determining the taxation of Social Security benefits is described in Ill. 9.9.)

What is important to emphasize is that for this purpose, income includes both earned and investment income, taxable and tax free. In other words, interest from savings accounts, CDs, corporate bonds and municipal bonds all counts toward the thresholds. If income exceeds these step-rate thresholds, up to 85 percent of the Social Security benefit could be taxed.

To the extent that investment income is not needed to fund retirement, an annuity can help protect a retired individual from the taxation of his or her Social Security benefits. To illustrate this, consider an example. Joe, who is married, has $400,000 invested in income-producing investments, some taxable, some tax free. These investments generate $29,000 a year in income ($300,000 at 8 percent [taxable] and $100,000 at 5 percent [tax free]). In addition, Joe receives a $25,000 pension and a $10,000 Social Security benefit. For purposes of the Social Security benefit tax, Joe's income is $59,000—the interest income plus his pension plus one-half of his Social Security benefit. (See Ill. 9.10.)

---

**ILL. 9.9 ■ *Formula for Determining Taxation of Social Security Benefits***

---

**Step 1:** Determine modified AGI (total of earnings, pension benefits, dividends and taxable and tax-free interest from investments and other sources, plus 50 percent of Social Security benefits)

**Step 2:** Determine excess of modified AGI over first threshold ($25,000 for single filers; $32,000 for joint filers)

**Step 3:** Determine excess of modified AGI over second threshold ($34,000 for single filers; $44,000 for joint filers)

**Step 4:** Determine smallest of:

    a. 50 percent of excess over first threshold, plus 35 percent of excess over second threshold

        or

    b. 85 percent of Social Security benefits

        or

    c. 50 percent of Social Security benefits, plus 85 percent of excess over second threshold

The smallest of the three figures in Step 4 is the amount of Social Security benefits subject to tax. An example of this calculation is illustrated in Ill. 9.10.

---

But Joe doesn't need the $29,000 he receives as income from his investments. Currently, he's simply reinvesting those earnings. If he were to shift the $400,000 of investments into an annuity, the Social Security tax would be eliminated. Illustration 9.11 shows how this would be accomplished.

There are many variations to this concept which can be tailored to meet the needs and circumstances of the individual prospect. The key to remember is that most individuals hate to pay taxes, especially when it comes to their Social Security benefits.

## ■ ANNUITY ILLUSTRATIONS

Because the annuity is an investment product, it lends itself to be sold by illustration and projections. And because of market conduct issues and the potential for misuse of product illustrations, intentional or not, extreme care must be taken with respect to what can and should be illustrated and projected.

## ILL. 9.10 ■ *Taxation of Social Security Benefits*

| | | |
|---|---|---|
| 1. | Modified AGI | |
| | Pension benefit | $25,000 |
| | 50 percent of Social Security benefit | $ 5,000 |
| | Investment income | |
| | $300,000 @ 8 percent | $24,000 |
| | $100,000 @ 5 percent | $ 5,000 |
| | Total | $59,000 |
| 2. | Excess of income over first threshold of $32,000 ($59,000 – $32,000) | $27,000 |
| 3. | Excess of income over second threshold of $44,000 ($59,000 – $44,000) | $15,000 |
| 4. | Determine the smallest of | |
| | a. 50 percent of excess over first threshold plus 35 percent of excess over second threshold ([.50 x $27,000] + [.35 x $15,000]) | $18,750 |
| | b. 85 percent of Social Security benefits | $ 8,500 |
| | c. 50 percent of Social Security benefits plus 85 percent of excess over second threshold [$5,000 + (.85 x $15,000)] | $17,750 |
| 5. | Amount of Social Security benefit subject to tax (smallest of a, b or c in Step 4) | $ 8,500 |

### Variable Annuities

For variable annuities, this issue has been addressed by the NASD, which has established standards that practitioners must adhere to when creating illustrations and proposals. Because these illustrations and proposals (or more likely, the software programs that generate them) are provided by the insurer, the practitioner does not have to be overly concerned with them in practice. As background, though, some information is useful.

A proposal or illustration cannot show growth in a variable annuity and compare it to a nontax-deferred investment unless the annuity is also shown on an after-tax basis in the same illustration. Hypothetical performance cannot be used to illustrate future values. However, an assumed interest rate can be used to project values into the future. Past performance of a subaccount can be used to illustrate a retrospective picture.

**ILL. 9.11 ■ *Eliminating the Taxation of Social Security Benefits***

| | Without an Annuity | With an Annuity |
|---|---|---|
| Income | | |
| Pension | $25,000 | $25,000 |
| Includable Social Security benefits | $ 5,000 | $ 5,000 |
| Investment Income | | |
| $300,000 @ 8 percent | $24,000 | $0* |
| $100,000 @ 5 percent | $ 5,000 | $0* |
| Annuity earnings @ 8 percent | | $32,000 |
| Total income and earnings | $59,000 | $62,000 |
| Income included in Social Security benefit calculation | $59,000 | $30,000 *(Amount is below the threshold for taxation of Social Security benefits for joint filers)* |
| Social Security benefit subject to tax | $ 8,500 | $0 |
| Taxes on Social Security benefit @ 31 percent | $ 2,635 | $0 |

*It should be noted that actually Joe's Social Security benefit tax would have been eliminated by shifting only $360,000 of his investments into an annuity.

### Fixed Annuities

For fixed annuities, there is currently no regulatory body that has developed guidelines for illustrations. This is of some concern, given the growth of equity-indexed annuities and the need to be able to illustrate the value of the concept. However, the NAIC has created a working group to study the issue and to try and develop standards for illustrations that are consistent with the work done by the NASD.

### ■ SUMMARY

In this chapter, we have reviewed the annuity market in terms of market definition and product uses. Of particular importance is the need to recognize that there are a multitude of ways to define and segment the market and the uses of the product. As time goes by, market definition will become more and more refined, and research techniques will continue to improve, enabling more effective evaluation of the markets. In addition, the design of the annuity itself will continue to evolve and change, creating ever-increasing uses and applications for this unique product. This proves again the dynamic nature of the annuity market.

■ **CHAPTER 9 QUESTIONS FOR REVIEW**

1. Geo-demographics attempts to apply geographic sensitivity to demographic principles.

   *True* or *False*

2. Segmentation is a method of focusing sales efforts by selectively eliminating unqualified buyers.

   *True* or *False*

3. Interest credited to an annuity, while in deferral, is not included as income when making calculations to determine taxation of Social Security benefits.

   *True* or *False*

4. The average age of the single-premium, nonqualified fixed annuity buyer is

   a. 45.
   b. 58.
   c. 38.
   d. 52.

5. All of the following are annuity characteristics that consumers look for, EXCEPT:

   a. safety.
   b. tax deferral.
   c. probate avoidance.
   d. short-term investment.

# 10

# Annuity Investment Management

U ntil a few years ago, no one really seemed to care how insurance companies invested the funds of their annuity contractholders, as long as the credited interest rates were high relative to other investment alternatives. But like everything else, times have changed. Concern by practitioners and consumers alike in how annuity monies are invested has come to the forefront in an era of junk bonds, delinquent mortgages and problem real estate. The press has made the public very aware of some of the problems associated with insurance company investments. Because of the fall of insurance companies like Executive Life, First Capital and Mutual Benefit, and because of the rating agencies, a new and appropriate spotlight has been directed onto the insurance industry in general, and investment-oriented insurance products specifically. In this chapter, we will look at how insurers invest for annuities and how this affects the products a producer brings to the market.

■ ■ ■ ■ ■

## ■ CASH FLOW CHARACTERISTICS OF ANNUITIES

Before we discuss how insurers invest for annuities, we have to remind ourselves of what an annuity is and how it works. First and foremost, from an investment standpoint, an annuity is an asset-management product. In other words, contractholders place their money with an insurance company, where it is pooled with money from other contractholders, with the expectation that the insurer can earn a return higher than what the contractholders could have earned on their own.

Out of this higher return, the insurer must pay its costs—including commissions—and earn a profit. All the while the insurer must be able to give back to any contractholder his or her money, whenever it may be requested, without incurring losses. Depending on product design, this is not always possible. Therefore, part of the insurer's task is to minimize the opportunities for contractholders to get money at inopportune times and thus minimize its own risk of *disintermediation*.

Basically, there are four ways contractholders can take their money out of an annuity: through death, free withdrawals, surrenders (partial or total) and annuitization. Each of these presents its own challenge to the insurer.

## Managing the Death Risk

Most annuity products provide for payment of the total account value to the policy's designated beneficiary at the death of the annuitant or contractholder. Payment of total account value means that no surrender charges or other adjustments are imposed on the account. The insurer must price the product for this contingency, called the *mortality risk*. Basically, it's the risk that the annuitant or owner will die before the insurer has recovered its costs of issuing and selling the annuity. Mortality risk can also be the risk that the owner or annuitant will die before the insurer's assets have reached maturity and have suffered a loss of market value. This would typically occur in a rising-rate environment.

Most insurers manage the mortality risk through three methods. First, they invest the money in assets (described later in this chapter) that provide for some liquidity in the early years to satisfy this requirement. Next, they price the product as necessary to recover the losses on these early deaths. In other words, much like a life insurance policy, those who are living will pay for the policy losses on those who have died. In the case of a deferred annuity, the living contractholders will pay by getting slightly lower credited rates. The third way insurers manage the mortality risk is to avoid it. To avoid the risk, insurers minimize the number of annuities they write on individuals whose life expectancy is less than the break-even point. This is generally done by either limiting the maximum age of the contractholder and/or annuitant (usual limits are age 70 to 80) or reducing commissions on contracts issued past a certain age. Most often, both of these methods are used.

## Managing the Free Withdrawal Risk

As we have learned, most deferred annuities allow for a limited free withdrawal every year. Typically the amount of the withdrawal is 10 percent of the accumulated account value and no surrender charges or other adjustments are imposed if this right is exercised. The insurer must be in a position to manage this risk profitably.

Over the last decade or so, contractholders as a whole have not exercised this right very frequently. In fact, some insurer studies have shown that less than 1 percent of annuity assets are distributed in this manner. That has been good for insurers, because they've been able to realize their spreads on 99 percent of assets instead of 90 percent, resulting (in theory) in 10 percent higher profits. However, it is unlikely that this will always be the case. The past 10 years have been a period of generally falling interest rates. As such, few contractholders would benefit from utilizing the

10 percent free withdrawal if their intent was to find a higher interest rate. However, if the reverse were to occur, there would most certainly be a much higher rate of disintermediation. In other words, if market interest rates were to increase, contractholders might wish to access their accounts and put 10 percent of the account value in an alternative product or perhaps another annuity at a higher rate. However, one aspect of such a transaction that might discourage contractholders from doing this is that they would be incurring a taxable event. As you will learn in the next chapter, partial "like-kind" 1035 exchanges are not tax advantaged and are fully taxable (unlike full exchanges).

How carriers manage this free withdrawal risk is discussed in detail later, but in essence they must choose investment vehicles that release enough cash annually to satisfy anticipated demand.

## Managing the Surrender Risk

Nearly all annuities allow contractholders to surrender their policies, fully or in part. Even the nonsurrenderable annuity certificates discussed in Chapter 5 allow for full surrenders at the end of the initial guarantee period. Generally speaking, satisfying the demand of full or partial surrenders during the surrender charge period has not been a major concern of insurers. Unlike a free withdrawal, full or partial surrenders are penalized to the extent of any applicable surrender charges. This provides the insurer some level of protection against disintermediation. Partial surrenders, again because they do not receive 1035 tax-free exchange treatment, also carry the additional discouraging factor of taxability.*

Yet surrenders, especially full surrenders, do carry a risk to the insurer. The insurer must be in a position to satisfy the liquidity demands of full surrenders, especially in the waning years of surrender charges. A 1 percent or 2 percent surrender charge will not be much of a deterrent to a contractholder who questions the safety of the current insurer or who has an opportunity to receive a 3 percent or 4 percent higher interest rate from a competing insurer. This is precisely why the insurer must have liquidity equal to or greater than the liquidity that could be demanded by its contractholders. As noted, insurers have not experienced much disintermediation because rates have generally declined over the last decade. Obviously, that trend won't last forever.

## Managing the Annuitization Risk

The cash flow characteristics of annuitization are probably the easiest of all for the insurer to manage. Generally speaking, when individuals annuitize their deferred annuity contracts, they do so over some period based on their lifetime. To an

---

*It should be noted that as a result of recent legislation, partial exchanges are allowed from TSAs. These exchanges are called *9024 exchanges*.

insurance company, a "lifetime" is a quantifiable period; life expectancy is a factor an insurer understands. Consequently, the insurer experiences no shock surrender or payout whereby it has to satisfy immediate and unpredicted liquidity. It has an opportunity to pay out the money over at least five years (the usual minimum annuitization period) and most probably, over the individual's lifetime. More important though is that when death occurs during the life-only annuitization phase, payment stops altogether, whereas when death occurs during the deferral stage, 100 percent payout must be made to the beneficiary. These important cash flow characteristics of annuitization are why insurers encourage it as a distribution option.

### Managing Cash Flow

The previous discussion of the cash flow characteristics of annuities focused on cash *outflow*. Cash *inflow*, a somewhat more simple concept, must also be considered.

Annuity cash inflow is what the insurer receives in premiums. It usually takes one of two forms: single premium (with all the money coming in at once) or flexible premium (with the money coming in over a period of months or years). Single premium is the more easily managed since the insurer knows how much money it will have to invest and can postpone any decisions or investment commitments until the money is in hand. Flexible premium products present a more interesting challenge with regard to predicting how long or to what degree the monies will continue to flow. Many economic factors will influence this cash flow: market interest rates, insurer interest rates, recessionary conditions, insurer publicity and tax law. An insurer must be prepared to handle the changes created by these different cash flow scenarios.

### ■ ASSET-LIABILITY MATCHING

Now that we've evaluated the potential for inflow and outflow, we're ready to discuss the consequences. Numerous studies over the past five years have shown that the most significant potential problem facing insurance companies is not junk bonds, not problem real estate, not delinquent mortgages, but *asset-liability matching*. First, let's define what we mean by asset-liability matching (sometimes called "asset-liability management").

When an insurance company receives money from an individual contractholder, those funds become a liability for the insurer. In other words, though the company has possession of the funds, they really don't belong to the insurer; they belong to the contractholder and will eventually have to be repaid. Once received, the insurer then takes that money and invests it.

The most common way of investing annuity monies is to purchase corporate bonds. The insurer pools all the premium deposits that arrive in a given period of time and invests them by buying a part of a new issue of a corporate bond. The insurer now owns a corporate bond—this bond becomes an asset of the insurance company.

However, this is where it gets more difficult. The insurer should be certain that the cash flow characteristics of the asset (bond) match, or are able to be matched, to those of the liability (annuity). Therefore, the average duration of the bond should be less than or equal to the average duration of the annuity. (For simplicity, we'll define duration of a bond as the length of time it is held by the insurer before it matures or is called, though this is technically only correct for zero-coupon bonds.) Not only must the duration be matched, but so must the cash flow characteristics during the lifetime of both the assets and liabilities. An example of this would be having the cash flow necessary to satisfy free withdrawals or partial surrenders, without having to sell the bond.

Most insurers match their cash flow needs with multiple bonds in staggered maturities. Some bonds may mature in one to two years while others may mature a year or two beyond the surrender charge period. That's why it's important to look at the average duration of the entire portfolio to compare against the length of the surrender charge period.

### A Well-Matched Asset and Liability

Illustration 10.1 shows a well-matched asset and liability. Note that the 8.5 percent coupon (the annual interest paid to the bondholder) results in $85,000 of bond cash flow that can be used to satisfy free withdrawal demand and partially used to satisfy

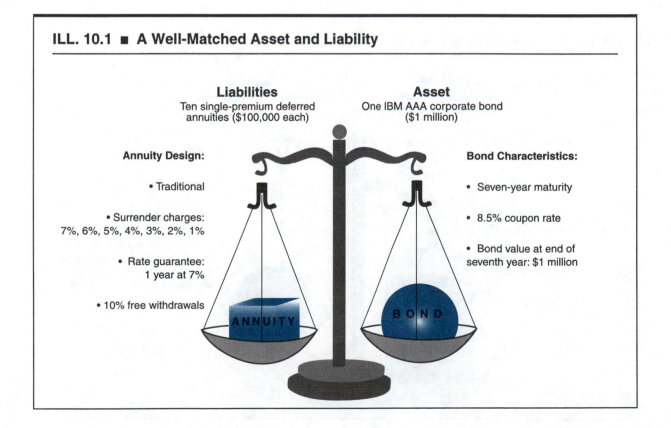

**ILL. 10.1 ■ A Well-Matched Asset and Liability**

**Liabilities**
Ten single-premium deferred annuities ($100,000 each)

**Asset**
One IBM AAA corporate bond ($1 million)

**Annuity Design:**

• Traditional

• Surrender charges:
7%, 6%, 5%, 4%, 3%, 2%, 1%

• Rate guarantee:
1 year at 7%

• 10% free withdrawals

**Bond Characteristics:**

• Seven-year maturity

• 8.5% coupon rate

• Bond value at end of seventh year: $1 million

early surrenders. Early surrenders will also be penalized with surrender charges, giving the insurer the opportunity to recover for early surrenders from those charges as well. The insurer will credit $70,000 per year in interest to the annuities. Realize that this is not really a cash flow requirement; it's merely a crediting requirement. Contractholders will not receive the yearly interest in cash; instead it will remain in the account and grow at a compound rate. Therefore, this can be ignored as a cash flow requirement until a full surrender occurs. Most important, at the time the insurer has the greatest risk of shock surrenders—year 10—all of the monies are mature and available to cover such a contingency.

Obviously the insurer hopes it will not be faced with any mass surrenders at that time, as it probably has not held the money long enough to earn much of a profit. Typically, an insurer needs to hold 50 percent of the deposits for 12 to 15 years to meet profit targets. The 1.5 percent target spread between the bond rate and the annuity credited rate is not all profit. A significant portion of this goes toward covering initial sales costs (primarily commissions) and ongoing maintenance costs.

## A Mismatched Asset and Liability

Illustration 10.2 shows one of the most severe consequences of mismatching assets and liabilities. If interest rates increase by three percentage points over the next seven years, the insurer will experience a 15 percent loss on the bond. Unfortunately, the

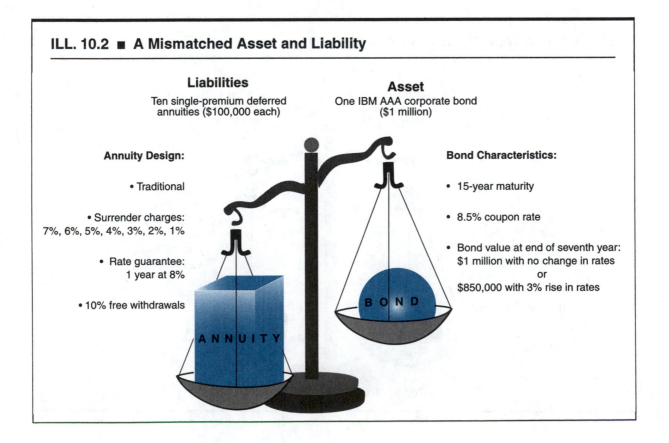

**ILL. 10.2 ■ A Mismatched Asset and Liability**

**Liabilities**
Ten single-premium deferred annuities ($100,000 each)

**Asset**
One IBM AAA corporate bond ($1 million)

**Annuity Design:**

• Traditional

• Surrender charges: 7%, 6%, 5%, 4%, 3%, 2%, 1%

• Rate guarantee: 1 year at 8%

• 10% free withdrawals

**Bond Characteristics:**

• 15-year maturity

• 8.5% coupon rate

• Bond value at end of seventh year: $1 million with no change in rates
or
$850,000 with 3% rise in rates

coupon rate will not be changing and the insurer will have little flexibility to credit a rate higher than 7 percent. However, since prevailing annuity rates at that point will be 10 percent, a major portion of the contractholders will leave to find higher rates. To accommodate these contractholders, the insurer will have to liquidate the bond at a 15 percent loss. This could have catastrophic consequences. Unfortunately, many insurers who have invested long in order to credit an attractive initial rate find themselves in this position today. The results of mismatching these portfolios will not be pleasant if the economy experiences moderate to significant interest rate increases over the next 5 to 10 years.

## Certificate Annuities

A special mention should be made regarding asset-liability matching on certificate annuities. Because of the special design of certificate annuities, whereby the contractholder has a predefined limited opportunity to surrender at certain intervals, asset-liability matching becomes much more critical. The insurer must be prepared to offer a new competitive rate of interest at the window times or risk abnormally high full surrenders that will be satisfied only by selling bonds at a loss.

## Equity-Indexed Annuities

The proliferation of equity-indexed annuities has done more to change the landscape of annuity investing than any product in recent history. Asset-liability matching is as important as ever, but both the assets and liabilities are very different from traditional annuity assets and liabilities. The basic difference revolves around the fact that the liability (annuity) must credit some equity market return. Therefore, so must the asset. A traditional bond will not do this. Additionally, the liability (annuity) must also provide for no losses. This truly complicates matters. Essentially, the insurer must find an asset that has stock market return with no downside risk.

Since no such vehicle exists, the insurer must build one. Illustration 10.3 shows how this is done. The guarantee side of the equation is accomplished with bonds. The insurer will use whatever portion of the initial premium is required to guarantee return of principal and minimum interest at the end of the guarantee period. The insurer sets aside the necessary amount to cover issuing costs, commissions and profits. Whatever is left over from the initial premium is then available for use in funding an equity-hedging instrument. The equity-hedging instrument will then guarantee certain performance in the stock market. The amount of money directed toward this instrument will determine the degree of market participation (usually called "participation percentage").

It's beyond the scope of this text to describe hedging instruments used as equity-indexed annuities, but they do perform similarly to call options. Normally, they are purchased from large international investment banks. It's important to evaluate where and how an insurer establishes this hedge such that the asset supports the liability.

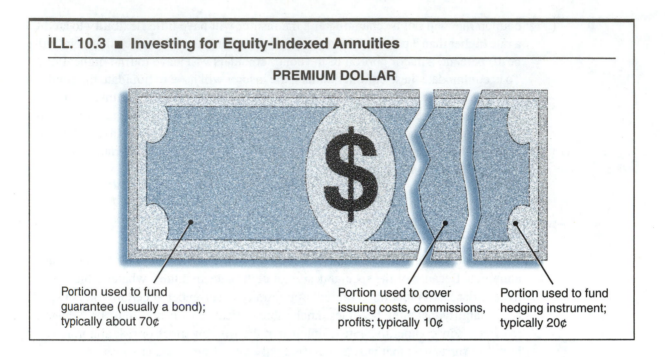

**ILL. 10.3 ■ Investing for Equity-Indexed Annuities**

**PREMIUM DOLLAR**

Portion used to fund guarantee (usually a bond); typically about 70¢

Portion used to cover issuing costs, commissions, profits; typically 10¢

Portion used to fund hedging instrument; typically 20¢

### Asset-Liability Matching: A Critical Component

One last point on asset-liability matching: some maintain that asset-liability matching is not that critical because the insurer can simply use current premium flow to satisfy surrenders from annuities that are already in force; however, this type of thinking is seriously flawed. Not only does it violate some insurance regulations, but it could most certainly turn a serious loss into a true catastrophe. The insurer would be turning one mismatch into another more severe mismatch as it tries to attract deposits at high rates backed by "old" assets at low rates.

### ■ ANNUITY INVESTMENT PHILOSOPHY

There are as many different investment philosophies regarding annuities as there are insurance companies. However, there is enough in common for us to evaluate some typical approaches to annuity investing.

### Bonds

As has been noted, by far the most common assets backing annuity contracts are bonds. There are many types of bonds and bond-like instruments. While it's beyond the scope of this text to evaluate all of these, the practitioner should be able to recognize some fundamental characteristics of treasuries, corporates, zero-coupon bonds, collateralized mortgage obligations (CMOs), collateralized bond obligations (CBOs), etc. All of these either are bonds or work like bonds to achieve what is necessary to satisfy the demands of a contractholder. Except for zeros, all bonds provide for some level of predictable yearly cash flow to satisfy free withdrawals and early surrenders. Bonds also provide for a guaranteed payback of principal at some predetermined time in the future. Certain bonds may be able to be "called" (i.e., paid off early by the bond issuer) before their scheduled maturity. These present a special problem, because an insurer could be counting on a high return for a long period of time, but instead find its expectations shattered because of a falling interest rate environment that makes it economically attractive for the bond issuer to pay off early. Insurers must be prepared for this eventuality either through pricing or by demanding some call protection on a portion of the portfolio.

Generally speaking, if the insurer buys private placements, any demands for call protection and other unique features can be more easily negotiated than in the open market. A private placement is a bond issue that is privately negotiated between the insurer and the bond issuer. There are no open market bids or ratings. This gives the insurer some significant leverage in bond character design to meet its specific needs and desires.

### Bond Ratings

All bonds are rated by the NAIC rating system. This system now closely parallels other rating services such as Standard & Poor's and Moody's. One major exception is that Standard & Poor's and Moody's do not rate private placements; this is only done by the NAIC system. Illustration 10.4 outlines the NAIC ratings method and compares it to Standard & Poor's and Moody's.

---

### ILL. 10.4 ■ *Bond Ratings*

| NAIC | Standard & Poor's | Moody's | Description |
|---|---|---|---|
| Class 1 | AAA, AA, A | Aaa, Aa, A | High-grade to medium-grade investment bonds. Capacity to repay principal and interest judged very high (AAA, Aaa) to slightly susceptible to adverse economic conditions (A, A). |
| Class 2 | BBB | Baa | Adequate capacity to repay principal and interest. Slightly speculative. |
| Class 3 | BB | Ba | Speculative. Significant chances that issuer could miss an interest payment. |
| Class 4 | B | B | Issuer has missed one or more interest or principal payments. |
| Class 5 | CCC, CC, C | Caa, Ca, C | Highly speculative to poor-quality issues that are in danger of default. C ratings mean no interest is being paid on the bond at this time. |
| Class 6 | Default | Default | Issuer is in default. Payment of interest or principal is in arrears. |

On average, life insurers maintain about 60 percent of their investment portfolio in bonds. Insurers that write significant amounts of annuities will typically have 75 percent or more of their annuity portfolio in bonds. Many insurers feel that since bonds represent such a natural match for annuity products, 90 percent or more of their portfolios should consist of bonds.

### Mortgages

The second most popular method of backing annuity policies is with *mortgages* or *mortgage pools*. Typically mortgage portfolios will represent 5 percent to 30 percent of an insurer's investment portfolio. Mortgages have some similarities to bonds in that some amount of cash flow is provided to the insurer every year in the form of interest and principal payment.

Mortgages are reasonably good matches for annuity portfolios, but they have one rather distinct disadvantage when compared to bonds. The cash flow is far less predictable. During recessionary times, default and delinquency rates rise rather significantly on mortgages. The impact is much more pronounced than on high-grade bonds. Perhaps a more important disadvantage is that during periods of falling interest rates, mortgages tend to be refinanced. There is not much an insurer can do to protect against that. Unfortunately, it occurs at exactly the wrong time—just when the company is counting on a high return, it is given back its investment and is forced to invest it elsewhere, at a lower rate.

Another important point about mortgage-backed annuities is that there is no NAIC rating. Therefore, practitioners and consumers alike are unable to have an independent expert evaluate the quality of a mortgage portfolio.

### Real Estate and Stocks

Practically speaking, neither real estate nor common stock represents a good match for annuity portfolios. There is no certain liquidity and no predictable cash flow. It is interesting to note, however, that many insurers are seeing an increase in their real estate portfolio as problem mortgages go into default and the company is forced to foreclose, thus owning the underlying property (collateral).

## ■ SUMMARY

Most of the discussion in this chapter centered around how insurers invest for the traditional annuity and the equity-indexed annuity. As we discussed in Chapter 5, however, there are many other types of annuity designs as well. Each of these designs would result in some minor variation to the traditional investment philosophy. The fully indexed interest design, for example, would have a substantially different philosophy from what was discussed here. This product requires hedging instruments such as caps or swaps. Discussion of these methods is well beyond the scope of this book; however, those who are involved in the sale and distribution of such products should have a working knowledge of these investment techniques.

■ **CHAPTER 10 QUESTIONS FOR REVIEW**

1. All bonds rated by the NAIC are also rated by Duff & Phelps.

   *True* or *False*

2. A bond maturing in 30 years represents a perfect investment for a five-year certificate annuity because of the high interest rate.

   *True* or *False*

3. For insurers writing substantial annuity business, their mortgage investments represent on average

   a. more than 70 percent of their total investments.
   b. less than 5 percent of their total investments.
   c. twice their bond portfolio.
   d. less than 30 percent of their total investments.

4. Many recent studies have shown that the most significant problem facing annuity insurers today is

   a. asset-liability matching.
   b. contractholders dying prematurely.
   c. contractholders not exercising their free withdrawal privilege.
   d. assets that are invested too short.

5. All of the following are reasons why a contractholder may be discouraged from taking a partial surrender from an annuity, EXCEPT:

   a. surrender charges.
   b. ordinary income tax.
   c. alternative safe investments have lower yields.
   d. alternative safe investments have higher yields.

# 11

# Annuity Taxation and Ownership

I n this final chapter we will explore the subject of annuity taxation and how it affects the structure of the contract. Since the early 1980s, there have been numerous pieces of legislation that have affected how annuities are treated. It is virtually impossible to detail every piece of legislation, regulation or private letter ruling that has affected annuities over the last 15 years. Therefore, we will focus on the highlights of major tax law provisions. It should be noted that even on some of these major provisions there is disagreement among tax professionals as to their meaning. Therefore, advisors should consult competent tax counsel prior to advising clients in any of the areas discussed. In most cases, any annuities sold prior to the change dates have been grandfathered and are not subject to the subsequent rules.

■ ■ ■ ■ ■

## ■ ANNUITY TAX LEGISLATION

To market and sell annuities effectively, the practitioner must understand the tax aspects of these products and how they might affect contractholders. In the first section of this chapter, we will look at how annuities are taxed and the implications that different income and liquidity options hold for contractholders from a tax standpoint. Over the years, the changes in the tax laws have served to encourage individuals to use annuities as retirement planning vehicles and discourage their use as short-term tax-sheltered investments. Let's begin by taking a brief look at the history of annuity tax legislation over the past 15 years.

### 1982—TEFRA

The *Tax Equity and Fiscal Responsibility Act of 1982* (TEFRA) was really the first significant piece of legislation to have an impact on annuities. Actually, the initial consensus was that the impact of TEFRA was so severe that the annuity market would dry up and go away. Obviously, that hasn't happened.

Prior to 1982, any withdrawal or distribution from an annuity before its maturity date was treated very favorably. The contractholder was allowed to recoup fully his or her invested principal first before any interest was deemed to be distributed. Since a return of principal is not taxed, this meant that contractholders could receive annuity withdrawals tax free until they had fully recovered the amounts they had invested. Any withdrawals beyond that represented interest, which is fully taxed. This approach to taxing withdrawals is known as "first-in, first-out" (FIFO)—that which is first put in (principal) is considered first to be paid out.

For example, assume Joe purchased a deferred annuity in 1978 for $100,000 and by 1981, it had grown to $130,000. If in 1981, Joe withdrew $25,000, that amount was considered to be a partial return of what he first put in (principal), not what was later put in (interest). Therefore, there were no income tax consequences to this withdrawal. In fact, Joe would have incurred no income tax consequences at all until his withdrawals reached $100,000. In essence, Joe had an opportunity to use his annuity as a tax-free income generator for some period of time.

In 1981, interest rates were at an all-time high, as were annuity sales. Then Congress stepped in. This use of annuities, they felt, was abusive and they took two steps to stem the flow.

### FIFO to LIFO

The first step was to change the tax treatment of annuity distributions from "first-in, first-out" to "last-in, first-out" (LIFO). This means that any distribution prior to maturity will now be treated as first a return of taxable interest, until all interest is recovered, and only then will nontaxable principal, or basis, be recovered. Using the example above, the $25,000 withdrawal would be considered a 100 percent taxable distribution of interest earnings. It is not hard to understand the significant impact this change had on annuities.

### Penalty on Interest Withdrawal

As significant as this change was, however, Congress wasn't done. They also imposed a 5 percent penalty on any interest withdrawal a contractholder took before the age of 59½, except for those taken in the event of death or disability, over a five-year (or longer) period or in cases where the annuity was held for at least 10 years prior to the distribution. Now, not only was the distribution taxable, but it was also subject to a potential 5 percent penalty.

The good news was that any annuity issued prior to the effective date of August 14, 1982, was grandfathered from these TEFRA regulations and remains so today.

### 1984—DEFRA

The *Deficit Reduction Act of 1984* (DEFRA) also affected annuities, though the impact was not quite as significant. The Deficit Reduction Act changed one of the exceptions to the 5 percent penalty tax. Specifically, it disallowed the 10-year holding period exception. This act also provided that distributions must be made from any deferred annuity at the time of the contractholder's or annuitant's death. This was an entirely new concept, as previous annuity ownership could be passed by will, allowing for multigeneration tax deferral. Once again, the good news was that any annuity issued prior to January 1, 1985, was grandfathered from these DEFRA rules.

### 1986—TRA

The *Tax Reform Act of 1986* (TRA), a major piece of tax legislation, once again changed the tax treatment for annuities. The penalty for pre-59½ distributions was raised from 5 percent to 10 percent and another exception to the penalty—the five-year payout exception—was disallowed. This meant that the penalty for pre-59½ distributions was 10 percent and the only exceptions were distributions taken at death, disability or as payment over life expectancy. The bad news is that there is no grandfather provision for these TRA 1986 changes.

The other significant effect this act imposed on annuities was to eliminate the tax-deferred inside build-up of corporate-owned annuities.

### 1988—TAMRA

The *Technical and Miscellaneous Reform Act of 1988* (TAMRA) had yet another change for annuities. Congress became aware of a practice that was meant to circumvent existing legislation. It was found, for example, that instead of buying one annuity contract for $100,000, individuals were buying ten $10,000 contracts. They would then take distributions from one contract, the amounts of which exceeded interest earnings credited to the one contract. This meant that these distributions would be deemed a return of principal and only partially taxed. Illustration 11.1 shows how multiple contracts would result in a $3,007 tax and penalty savings in the event of a hypothetical $7,000 distribution.

Obviously, Congress considered this to be abusive. Therefore, they instituted what has become known as the "aggregation rule." This rule states that all annuities purchased within one calendar year will be aggregated and treated as one contract for the purposes of determining taxation of withdrawals. The effective date of this requirement was October 22, 1988. Annuities purchased prior to that time are grandfathered from this provision.

### ILL. 11.1 ■ *Bypassing the Tax Law*

The following shows how purchasing multiple annuity contracts allowed contract-holders to circumvent the full effect of the tax law prior to 1988. Note the difference between the taxes, penalty and net distribution when a distribution was made from one $10,000 contract as opposed to a $100,000 contract. This example assumes the contractholder is age 55, and the interest rate credited to the annuities is 8 percent

| | Contractholder Buys One $100,000 Contract | Contractholder Buys Ten $10,000 Contracts |
|---|---|---|
| Account balance at end of one year: | $108,000 | $10,800 (× 10) |
| Distribution: | $7,000 | $7,000 |
| Amount of distribution that is taxable interest: | $7,000 | $800 |
| Amount of distribution that is nontaxable principal: | $0 | $6,200 |
| Tax on distribution (at 1987 rate of 38½ percent): | $2,695 | $308 |
| 10 percent penalty (assessed only on interest withdrawn): | $700 | $80 |
| Net distribution: | $3,605 | $6,612 |

The "aggregation rule," passed in 1988, treats all annuities purchased within one calendar year as one contract, for purposes of determining taxation of withdrawals. Consequently, the practice of taking withdrawals from multiple contacts is no longer tax advantaged.

### 1996—Small Business Act

The *Small Business Job Protection Act of 1996* contained a number of provisions related to qualified plans and pension simplification. It affected the taxation of qualified annuities by modifying the exclusion ratio formula used to determine plan participant basis and the nontaxable portion of qualified annuity payments. This modified exclusion ratio is explained later in this chapter.

## ■ GENERAL RULES OF ANNUITY TAXATION

The preceding discussion was included to give you an idea of the many changes that annuities have undergone over the past 15 years. As you can see, each new piece of legislation has had the effect of eroding some tax advantage to annuity ownership. It's essential that practitioners understand the impact of annuity tax legislation on their contractholders and prospects—who are or will be subject to the rules and the consequences of specific transactions.

Now let's pull it all together and see how annuities are taxed today. The following summarizes many points previously mentioned throughout the text.

## Taxation of Annuity Income

As first mentioned in Chapter 3, income received from a nonqualified annuity under a structured annuitization option is taxed in accordance with the *exclusion ratio*. The exclusion ratio treats each annuity payment as part principal and part interest, thereby excluding a portion of each payment from tax and taxing a portion. Recall that the exclusion ratio is the "investment in the contract" (i.e., total premiums paid) divided by the "expected return" (i.e., total amounts to be received). If the expected return is not based on a life expectancy—as would be the case with a fixed term of years option, for example—it is calculated simply by adding the total amounts to be received. If the expected return is based on a life (or joint life) expectancy, certain IRS-prescribed tables and multipliers are used to determine the total expected return. (See Ill. 11.2 and Ill. 11.3.) Let's look at an example.

This year Ray, age 60, purchases an immediate fixed annuity for $18,000 that will provide a guaranteed income of $150 a month for the rest of his life. As Ill. 11.2 shows, the expected return multiplier is 24.2. Ray's taxable and excludable annuity income would be calculated as follows:

| | |
|---|---|
| Investment in the contract: | $18,000 |
| Annual annuity payment ($150 × 12): | $ 1,800 |
| Multiplier: | 24.2 |
| Total expected return ($1,800 × 24.2): | $43,560 |
| Exclusion ratio ($18,000 ÷ $43,560): | 41.3% |
| Annual exclusion ($1,800 × .413): | $   743 |
| Annual taxable amount: | $ 1,057 |

Because his benefit is fixed and unchanging, Ray can continue to exclude the same amount each year until the total of all exclusions he has taken under the contract equals his $18,000 investment. After that, if Ray is still alive and receiving payments, each will be fully taxed.*

---

*It should be noted that contracts that annuitized prior to 1987 are allowed to carry an exclusion ratio indefinitely, no matter how long the annuitant lives or how much he or she receives in benefit payments. Thus, it's possible that these annuitants may receive tax free more than what they paid into the annuity. This permanent exclusion does not apply to annuities with a starting date after 1986.

## ILL. 11.2 ■ *Annuity Table V—Expected Return Multiples Ordinary Life Annuity—One Life*

| Age | Multiple | Age | Multiple | Age | Multiple |
|-----|----------|-----|----------|-----|----------|
| 5 | 76.6 | 42 | 40.6 | 79 | 10.0 |
| 6 | 75.6 | 43 | 39.6 | 80 | 9.5 |
| 7 | 74.7 | 44 | 38.7 | 81 | 8.9 |
| 8 | 73.7 | 45 | 37.7 | 82 | 8.4 |
| 9 | 72.7 | 46 | 36.8 | 83 | 7.9 |
| 10 | 71.7 | 47 | 35.9 | 84 | 7.4 |
| 11 | 70.7 | 48 | 34.9 | 85 | 6.9 |
| 12 | 69.7 | 49 | 34.0 | 86 | 6.5 |
| 13 | 68.8 | 50 | 33.1 | 87 | 6.1 |
| 14 | 67.8 | 51 | 32.2 | 88 | 5.7 |
| 15 | 66.8 | 52 | 31.3 | 89 | 5.3 |
| 16 | 65.8 | 53 | 30.4 | 90 | 5.0 |
| 17 | 64.8 | 54 | 29.5 | 91 | 4.7 |
| 18 | 63.9 | 55 | 28.6 | 92 | 4.4 |
| 19 | 62.9 | 56 | 27.7 | 93 | 4.1 |
| 20 | 61.9 | 57 | 26.8 | 94 | 3.9 |
| 21 | 60.9 | 58 | 25.9 | 95 | 3.7 |
| 22 | 59.9 | 59 | 25.0 | 96 | 3.4 |
| 23 | 59.0 | 60 | 24.2 | 97 | 3.2 |
| 24 | 58.0 | 61 | 23.3 | 98 | 3.0 |
| 25 | 57.0 | 62 | 22.5 | 99 | 2.8 |
| 26 | 56.0 | 63 | 21.6 | 100 | 2.7 |
| 27 | 55.1 | 64 | 20.8 | 101 | 2.5 |
| 28 | 54.1 | 65 | 20.0 | 102 | 2.3 |
| 29 | 53.1 | 66 | 19.2 | 103 | 2.1 |
| 30 | 52.2 | 67 | 18.4 | 104 | 1.9 |
| 31 | 51.2 | 68 | 17.6 | 105 | 1.8 |
| 32 | 50.2 | 69 | 16.8 | 106 | 1.6 |
| 33 | 49.3 | 70 | 16.0 | 107 | 1.4 |
| 34 | 48.3 | 71 | 15.3 | 108 | 1.3 |
| 35 | 47.3 | 72 | 14.6 | 109 | 1.1 |
| 36 | 46.4 | 73 | 13.9 | 110 | 1.0 |
| 37 | 45.4 | 74 | 13.2 | 111 | .9 |
| 38 | 44.4 | 75 | 12.5 | 112 | .8 |
| 39 | 43.5 | 76 | 11.9 | 113 | .7 |
| 40 | 42.5 | 77 | 11.2 | 114 | .6 |
| 41 | 41.5 | 78 | 10.6 | 115 | .5 |

This is a "unisex table," to be used if the "investment in the contract" includes any premiums paid after June 30, 1986. Gender-based tables are used if the "investment in the contract" does not include any premiums paid after June 30, 1986.

## ILL. 11.3 ■ *Annuity Table VI (Partial)—Expected Return Multiples Ordinary Joint-Life and Last Survivor—Two Parts*

| Age | 35 | 36 | 37 | 38 | 39 | 40 | 41 | 42 | 43 | 44 | 45 | 46 | 47 | 48 | 49 | 50 |
|---|---|---|---|---|---|---|---|---|---|---|---|---|---|---|---|---|
| 35 | 54.0 | ... | ... | ... | ... | ... | ... | ... | ... | ... | ... | ... | ... | ... | ... | ... |
| 36 | 53.5 | 53.0 | ... | ... | ... | ... | ... | ... | ... | ... | ... | ... | ... | ... | ... | ... |
| 37 | 53.0 | 52.5 | 52.0 | ... | ... | ... | ... | ... | ... | ... | ... | ... | ... | ... | ... | ... |
| 38 | 52.6 | 52.0 | 51.5 | 51.0 | ... | ... | ... | ... | ... | ... | ... | ... | ... | ... | ... | ... |
| 39 | 52.2 | 51.6 | 51.0 | 50.5 | 50.0 | ... | ... | ... | ... | ... | ... | ... | ... | ... | ... | ... |
| 40 | 51.8 | 51.2 | 50.6 | 50.0 | 49.5 | 49.0 | ... | ... | ... | ... | ... | ... | ... | ... | ... | ... |
| 41 | 51.4 | 50.8 | 50.2 | 49.6 | 49.1 | 48.5 | 48.0 | ... | ... | ... | ... | ... | ... | ... | ... | ... |
| 42 | 51.1 | 50.4 | 49.8 | 49.2 | 48.6 | 48.1 | 47.5 | 47.0 | ... | ... | ... | ... | ... | ... | ... | ... |
| 43 | 50.8 | 50.1 | 49.5 | 48.8 | 48.2 | 47.6 | 47.1 | 46.6 | 46.0 | ... | ... | ... | ... | ... | ... | ... |
| 44 | 50.5 | 49.8 | 49.1 | 48.5 | 47.8 | 47.2 | 46.7 | 46.1 | 45.6 | 45.1 | ... | ... | ... | ... | ... | ... |
| 45 | 50.2 | 49.5 | 48.8 | 48.1 | 47.5 | 46.9 | 46.3 | 45.7 | 45.1 | 44.6 | 44.1 | ... | ... | ... | ... | ... |
| 46 | 50.0 | 49.2 | 48.5 | 47.8 | 47.2 | 46.5 | 45.9 | 45.3 | 44.7 | 44.1 | 43.6 | 43.1 | ... | ... | ... | ... |
| 47 | 49.7 | 49.0 | 48.3 | 47.5 | 46.8 | 46.2 | 45.5 | 44.9 | 44.3 | 43.7 | 43.2 | 42.6 | 42.1 | ... | ... | ... |
| 48 | 49.5 | 48.8 | 48.0 | 47.3 | 46.6 | 45.9 | 45.2 | 44.5 | 43.9 | 43.3 | 42.7 | 42.2 | 41.7 | 41.2 | ... | ... |
| 49 | 49.3 | 48.5 | 47.8 | 47.0 | 46.3 | 45.6 | 44.9 | 44.2 | 43.6 | 42.9 | 42.3 | 41.8 | 41.2 | 40.7 | 40.2 | ... |
| 50 | 49.2 | 48.4 | 47.6 | 46.8 | 46.0 | 45.3 | 44.6 | 43.9 | 43.2 | 42.6 | 42.0 | 41.4 | 40.8 | 40.2 | 39.7 | 39.2 |
| 51 | 49.0 | 48.2 | 47.4 | 46.6 | 45.8 | 45.1 | 44.3 | 43.6 | 42.9 | 42.2 | 41.6 | 41.0 | 40.4 | 39.8 | 39.3 | 38.7 |
| 52 | 48.8 | 48.0 | 47.2 | 46.4 | 45.6 | 44.8 | 44.1 | 43.3 | 42.6 | 41.9 | 41.3 | 40.6 | 40.0 | 39.4 | 38.8 | 38.3 |
| 53 | 48.7 | 47.9 | 47.0 | 46.2 | 45.4 | 44.6 | 43.9 | 43.1 | 42.4 | 41.7 | 41.0 | 40.3 | 39.7 | 39.0 | 38.4 | 37.9 |
| 54 | 48.6 | 47.7 | 46.9 | 46.0 | 45.2 | 44.4 | 43.6 | 42.9 | 42.1 | 41.4 | 40.7 | 40.0 | 39.3 | 38.7 | 38.1 | 37.5 |
| 55 | 48.5 | 47.6 | 46.7 | 45.9 | 45.1 | 44.2 | 43.4 | 42.7 | 41.9 | 41.2 | 40.4 | 39.7 | 39.0 | 38.4 | 37.7 | 37.1 |
| 56 | 48.3 | 47.5 | 46.6 | 45.8 | 44.9 | 44.1 | 43.3 | 42.5 | 41.7 | 40.9 | 40.2 | 39.5 | 38.7 | 38.1 | 37.4 | 36.8 |
| 57 | 48.3 | 47.4 | 46.5 | 45.6 | 44.8 | 43.9 | 43.1 | 42.3 | 41.5 | 40.7 | 40.0 | 39.2 | 38.5 | 37.8 | 37.1 | 36.4 |
| 58 | 48.2 | 47.3 | 46.4 | 45.5 | 44.7 | 43.8 | 43.0 | 42.1 | 41.3 | 40.5 | 39.7 | 39.0 | 38.2 | 37.5 | 36.8 | 36.1 |
| 59 | 48.1 | 47.2 | 46.3 | 45.4 | 44.5 | 43.7 | 42.8 | 42.0 | 41.2 | 40.4 | 39.6 | 38.8 | 38.0 | 37.3 | 36.6 | 35.9 |
| 60 | 48.0 | 47.1 | 46.2 | 45.3 | 44.4 | 43.6 | 42.7 | 41.9 | 41.0 | 40.2 | 39.4 | 38.6 | 37.8 | 37.1 | 36.3 | 35.6 |
| 61 | 47.9 | 47.0 | 46.1 | 45.2 | 44.3 | 43.5 | 42.6 | 41.7 | 40.9 | 40.0 | 39.2 | 38.4 | 37.6 | 36.9 | 36.1 | 35.4 |
| 62 | 47.9 | 47.0 | 46.0 | 45.1 | 44.2 | 43.4 | 42.5 | 41.6 | 40.8 | 39.9 | 39.1 | 38.3 | 37.5 | 36.7 | 35.9 | 35.1 |
| 63 | 47.8 | 46.9 | 46.0 | 45.1 | 44.2 | 43.3 | 42.4 | 41.5 | 40.6 | 39.8 | 38.9 | 38.1 | 37.3 | 36.5 | 35.7 | 34.9 |
| 64 | 47.8 | 46.8 | 45.9 | 45.0 | 44.1 | 43.2 | 42.3 | 41.4 | 40.5 | 39.7 | 38.8 | 38.0 | 37.2 | 36.3 | 35.5 | 34.8 |
| 65 | 47.7 | 46.8 | 45.9 | 44.9 | 44.0 | 43.1 | 42.2 | 41.3 | 40.4 | 39.6 | 38.7 | 37.9 | 37.0 | 36.2 | 35.4 | 34.6 |
| 66 | 47.7 | 46.7 | 45.8 | 44.9 | 44.0 | 43.1 | 42.2 | 41.3 | 40.4 | 39.5 | 38.6 | 37.8 | 36.9 | 36.1 | 35.2 | 34.4 |
| 67 | 47.6 | 46.7 | 45.8 | 44.8 | 43.9 | 43.0 | 42.1 | 41.2 | 40.3 | 39.4 | 38.5 | 37.7 | 36.8 | 36.0 | 35.1 | 34.3 |
| 68 | 47.6 | 46.7 | 45.7 | 44.8 | 43.9 | 42.9 | 42.0 | 41.1 | 40.2 | 39.3 | 38.4 | 37.6 | 36.7 | 35.8 | 35.0 | 34.2 |
| 69 | 47.6 | 46.6 | 45.7 | 44.8 | 43.8 | 42.9 | 42.0 | 41.1 | 40.2 | 39.3 | 38.4 | 37.5 | 36.6 | 35.7 | 34.9 | 34.1 |
| 70 | 47.5 | 46.6 | 45.7 | 44.7 | 43.8 | 42.9 | 41.9 | 41.0 | 40.1 | 39.2 | 38.3 | 37.4 | 36.5 | 35.7 | 34.8 | 34.0 |
| 71 | 47.5 | 46.6 | 45.6 | 44.7 | 43.8 | 42.8 | 41.9 | 41.0 | 40.1 | 39.1 | 38.2 | 37.3 | 36.5 | 35.6 | 34.7 | 33.9 |
| 72 | 47.5 | 46.6 | 45.6 | 44.7 | 43.7 | 42.8 | 41.9 | 40.9 | 40.0 | 39.1 | 38.2 | 37.3 | 36.4 | 35.5 | 34.6 | 33.8 |
| 73 | 47.5 | 46.5 | 45.6 | 44.7 | 43.7 | 42.8 | 41.8 | 40.9 | 40.0 | 39.0 | 38.1 | 37.2 | 36.3 | 35.4 | 34.6 | 33.7 |
| 74 | 47.5 | 46.5 | 45.6 | 44.7 | 43.7 | 42.7 | 41.8 | 40.9 | 39.9 | 39.0 | 38.1 | 37.2 | 36.3 | 35.4 | 34.5 | 33.6 |
| 75 | 47.4 | 46.5 | 45.5 | 44.7 | 43.6 | 42.7 | 41.8 | 40.8 | 39.9 | 39.0 | 38.1 | 37.1 | 36.2 | 35.3 | 34.5 | 33.6 |
| 76 | 47.4 | 46.5 | 45.5 | 44.7 | 43.6 | 42.7 | 41.7 | 40.8 | 39.9 | 38.9 | 38.0 | 37.1 | 36.2 | 35.3 | 34.4 | 33.5 |
| 77 | 47.4 | 46.5 | 45.5 | 44.7 | 43.6 | 42.7 | 41.7 | 40.8 | 39.8 | 38.9 | 38.0 | 37.1 | 36.2 | 35.3 | 34.4 | 33.5 |
| 78 | 47.4 | 46.4 | 45.5 | 44.5 | 43.6 | 42.6 | 41.7 | 40.7 | 39.8 | 38.9 | 38.0 | 37.0 | 36.1 | 35.2 | 34.3 | 33.4 |
| 79 | 47.4 | 46.4 | 45.5 | 44.5 | 43.6 | 42.6 | 41.7 | 40.7 | 39.8 | 38.9 | 37.9 | 37.0 | 36.1 | 35.2 | 34.3 | 33.4 |
| 80 | 47.4 | 46.4 | 45.5 | 44.5 | 43.6 | 42.6 | 41.7 | 40.7 | 39.8 | 38.8 | 37.9 | 37.0 | 36.1 | 35.2 | 34.2 | 33.4 |
| 81 | 47.4 | 46.4 | 45.5 | 44.5 | 43.5 | 42.6 | 41.6 | 40.7 | 39.8 | 38.8 | 37.9 | 37.0 | 36.0 | 35.1 | 34.2 | 33.3 |
| 82 | 47.4 | 46.4 | 45.4 | 44.5 | 43.5 | 42.6 | 41.6 | 40.7 | 39.7 | 38.8 | 37.9 | 36.9 | 36.0 | 35.1 | 34.2 | 33.3 |
| 83 | 47.4 | 46.4 | 45.4 | 44.5 | 43.5 | 42.6 | 41.6 | 40.7 | 39.7 | 38.8 | 37.8 | 36.9 | 36.0 | 35.1 | 34.2 | 33.2 |
| 84 | 47.4 | 46.4 | 45.4 | 44.5 | 43.5 | 42.6 | 41.6 | 40.7 | 39.7 | 38.8 | 37.8 | 36.9 | 36.0 | 35.0 | 34.1 | 33.2 |
| 85 | 47.4 | 46.4 | 45.4 | 44.5 | 43.5 | 42.6 | 41.6 | 40.7 | 39.7 | 38.8 | 37.8 | 36.9 | 36.0 | 35.0 | 34.1 | 33.2 |
| 86 | 47.3 | 46.4 | 45.4 | 44.5 | 43.5 | 42.5 | 41.6 | 40.6 | 39.7 | 38.8 | 37.8 | 36.9 | 36.0 | 35.0 | 34.1 | 33.2 |
| 87 | 47.3 | 46.4 | 45.4 | 44.5 | 43.5 | 42.5 | 41.6 | 40.6 | 39.7 | 38.7 | 37.8 | 36.9 | 35.9 | 35.0 | 34.1 | 33.2 |
| 88 | 47.3 | 46.4 | 45.4 | 44.5 | 43.5 | 42.5 | 41.6 | 40.6 | 39.7 | 38.7 | 37.8 | 36.9 | 35.9 | 35.0 | 34.1 | 33.2 |
| 89 | 47.3 | 46.4 | 45.4 | 44.4 | 43.5 | 42.5 | 41.6 | 40.6 | 39.7 | 38.7 | 37.8 | 36.9 | 35.9 | 35.0 | 34.1 | 33.2 |
| 90 | 47.3 | 46.4 | 45.4 | 44.4 | 43.5 | 42.5 | 41.6 | 40.6 | 39.7 | 38.7 | 37.8 | 36.9 | 35.9 | 35.0 | 34.1 | 33.2 |

This is a "unisex table," to be used if the "investment in the contract" includes any premiums paid after June 30, 1986. Gender-based tables are used if the "investment in the contract" does not include any premiums paid after June 30, 1986.

Annuity payments that vary from month to month or year to year—as variable annuities do—require slightly different calculations and follow a special rule to determine the portion of each payment that is "an amount received as an annuity" and excluded from tax. Also, in the case of joint-life or joint and survivor annuities, different tables and different multipliers are used, reflecting the ages of both annuitants. (See Ill. 11.3.) Annuities that contain a cash or installment refund feature also require different calculations. For one thing, when determining the exclusion, the investment in the contract must be adjusted downward to reflect the value of the refund as of the annuity starting date.

Finally, annuity payments received under a qualified plan are taxed according to a modified exclusion ratio formula. This is explained in Ill. 11.4.

---

### ILL. 11.4 ▪ *Modified Exclusion Ratio for Qualified Annuity Payments*

The Small Business Protection Act of 1996 created a simplified method of determining the nontaxable portion of qualified annuity payments (or other qualified periodic payments). This method modifies the exclusion ratio and uses the following formula:

$$\frac{\text{Participant's Investment in the Contract as of the Annuity Start Date}}{\text{Number of Anticipated Payments}}$$

The participant's "investment in the contract" would be the total premiums or contributions he or she made to the plan, less an amount received before the start date that was not included in gross income. The "number of anticipated payments" is based on the following chart, which assumes payments are monthly:

| Age of Primary Annuitant as of Annuity Starting Date | Number of Anticipated Payments |
|:---:|:---:|
| 55 and under | 360 |
| 56–60 | 310 |
| 61–65 | 260 |
| 66–70 | 210 |
| 71 and over | 160 |

For example, Betty contributed $20,000 to her qualified plan over the years. At 62, she retires and begins receiving a $350 per month pension payment. Under the modified exclusion ratio, the nontaxable portion of each monthly payment would be $76.92 ($20,000 ÷ 260); the balance would be taxable.

If the number of payments is fixed (as opposed to payments based on a life contingency), that number would be used as the denominator in the formula instead of the number of anticipated payments in the table. Also, if the payments are not made monthly, adjustments are to be made to reflect the period on which payments are based (annually, quarterly, etc.).

### Taxation to the Beneficiary at the Annuitant's Death (Post-Annuitization)

In cases where an annuitant owns a term certain or refund annuity and dies after payments begin but before receiving the full amount guaranteed, the balance is paid to a designated beneficiary. In these cases, the amounts paid to the beneficiary—whether as a single payment or in installments—are received tax free until the sum of all payments that were excluded from tax exceed total premiums invested. After that, any amounts the beneficiary receives are fully taxable.

### Taxation to the Beneficiary at the Annuitant's Death (Pre-Annuitization)

In cases where the owner is the same as the annuitant, what happens at the annuitant's death is governed by the rules applicable at the owner's death. In cases where the annuitant is different from the owner and the annuitant dies first, federal tax law does not require that taxes be paid *unless* the contract terminates, which many do. However, recent clarification on this issue by Congress and the IRS has given insurers confidence to design contracts that survive the death of a nonowner annuitant by naming a new annuitant. Often this is the owner or contingent annuitant.

One important exception to this occurs when the owner is a "non-natural" person, such as a trust. In these situations, the death of the annuitant results in exactly the same tax treatment as the death of an owner.

### Taxation to the Beneficiary at the Owner's Death

For contracts in deferral, federal tax law requires that any gain in the contract be recognized and consequent taxes paid whenever the owner dies. This is also true in the event of multiple owners when *any* owner dies. Therefore, most annuity contracts provide for payment of the death benefit to the beneficiary at the time of the owner's death. This means that the beneficiary will be responsible for income taxes on the contract's gain. Illustration 11.5 explains the options available to the beneficiary.

### Taxation of Annuity Withdrawals and Distributions

As we've discussed throughout this text, there are a number of ways for contractholders to access the values in their annuities other than through annuitization. These options include systematic withdrawals, loans and full or partial surrenders, all of which can be utilized before an annuity's maturity date. However, as pointed out at the beginning of this chapter, current tax laws are such that any of these distribution options may create a taxable event. Let's review the rules.

---

### ILL. 11.5 ■ *The History of the Annuity Death Benefit*

---

Traditionally, annuity contracts were written to provide payment of the death benefit upon the death of the annuitant because the annuitant's life was considered to be (and still is) the measuring life for purposes of annuity income payments. People were then able to derive multigenerational tax deferral by passing on annuity ownership by will. The Deficit Reduction Act of 1984 eliminated this loophole by amending the tax code to require that insurers distribute an annuity's contract value upon the death of the "holder." Though successful in its effort to eliminate the loophole, the new law confused many insurers by the use of the term "holder." In May of 1987, the Joint Committee on Taxation issued an explanation to the tax reform act, clarifying that the "holder" of an annuity contract was in fact the owner of the contract.

Under current tax law, if death of the owner occurs *after* the annuity starting date, any remaining annuity payments must be distributed to the beneficiary in a manner that is at least as rapid as the method that was in place prior to death. For example, say Bill, age 55, purchases an annuity contact and is the owner and annuitant; his son is named as the beneficiary. Bill annuitizes the contract at age 60 choosing a 10-year term certain income option. Unfortunately, Bill dies after receiving payments for only two years. His son, as named beneficiary, must receive the remaining annuity payments (or a sum equal to the present value of the remaining payments) before the eight-year period ends.

If death of the owner occurs *before* the annuity starting date, current tax law requires that the entire interest in the contract must be distributed within five years or by periodic payments that begin no later than December 31 of the year following the year of death. These payments are to be made over the beneficiary's expected life. For example, Susan, age 55, purchases an annuity contract and is the owner. She names her son as the annuitant. Upon Susan's death, the entire interest in the contract must be distributed within five years or the contract must be annuitized within one year of the date of death. (It is important to note that a surviving spouse of a deceased contract owner may continue the contract as the new owner, if the surviving spouse was the designated beneficiary of the contract.)

As a result of the change in tax law, some annuity contracts were revised to comply with these requirements, paying the *contract value* at death of the owner and paying the *death benefit* upon death of the annuitant. Understand that there can be a significant dollars and cents difference between the contract value and the death benefit. Many times the contract value is paid out less surrender charges and/or market value adjustments. In the case of variable annuities, a death benefit that guarantees the return of principal will exceed the contract value in the event of the owner's death during a market decline.

Recently there has been a trend to simplify annuity death benefit provisions, whereby insurers now provide solely for an owner death benefit unless a non-natural person is the owner. In these cases, the death of the annuitant would trigger the payment of the death benefit. In the event a nonowner annuitant predeceases the owner, many insurers allow the owner to become the annuitant or to name a new annuitant.

### Annuities Purchased Prior to August 14, 1982

For annuities purchased before August 14, 1982, the general rule regarding cash withdrawals, amounts received as loans or amounts received on surrenders is that they are tax free until they equal the contractholder's basis or investment in the contract. After that, they are fully taxable as income. These annuities are given "first-in, first-out" (FIFO) treatment.

### Annuities Purchased After August 14, 1982

For annuities purchased on or after August 14, 1982, the general rule regarding these same kinds of distributions is that they will be treated first as fully taxable interest payments and only second as a recovery of nontaxable basis. These annuities are given "last-in, first-out" (LIFO) treatment.

## Penalties for Early Distributions or Withdrawals

To promote the use of annuities as retirement plans and to discourage their use as short-term tax-sheltered investments, a 10 percent penalty is imposed on "premature" distributions, or those taken before the contractholder's age 59½. Therefore, an individual who, at age 54, withdraws a sum of $5,000 from his or her annuity will have to pay a current tax plus a $500 penalty as well, to the extent the withdrawal is attributed to interest earnings. No penalty is imposed for distributions taken:

- after age 59½;

- in the event of disability;

- in the event of death; or

- as part of a series of substantially equal payments taken over life expectancy.

## Estate Taxation of Annuities

A discussion of annuity taxation would not be complete without a reference to the estate tax consequences of these products. Actually, the rules are fairly straightforward. If the contractholder dies during the deferral period (prior to annuitization), the entire account value of the annuity is included in his or her gross estate for purposes of determining the estate tax. If the contractholder dies after annuitization has begun and payments continue to a beneficiary (under a term certain or survivor annuity), then the present value of those future payments is included in the contractholder's gross estate. If the annuitization election is the life-only option, then there is no value for estate tax purposes, since payments cease at the contractholder's death.

Again, it's essential for practitioners to understand the impact of annuity tax legislation on their clients, since they must be in a position to recommend the proper retirement or estate planning option. Much of the planning will focus on the impact of legislation on the structure of the annuity contract.

## ■ STRUCTURING THE ANNUITY CONTRACT

An annuity is a contract between the contractholder and the insurance company. But it also affects two other parties: the annuitant and the beneficiary. When we talk of contract structure, we refer to the decision regarding naming the annuitant and beneficiary. For those familiar with the nature of life insurance contracts, an easy analogy can be drawn: life insurance is to the owner-insured-beneficiary as an annuity is to the owner-annuitant-beneficiary. Let's take a closer look at these three parties.

### Owner

The *owner* of an annuity enters into a contract with the insurer. It is the owner who makes the premium deposits to buy the contract, and it is the owner who enjoys the tax deferral. As long as the owner is alive, only he or she can control decisions relating to the annuity. These decisions include annuitization, withdrawals, surrenders or changes in designating the annuitant or beneficiary. The owner's death will typically trigger a payment of all annuity accumulation value to the beneficiary. (Note spousal and other exceptions discussed next and in Ills. 11.5 and 11.6.)

In some cases, spouses want to own an annuity contract *jointly*. This is permissible by most insurers. In these cases, the practitioner must take care to advise the buyers that they should be designated as joint beneficiaries. Otherwise, if husband and wife are joint owners and a child is the beneficiary, a forced taxable distribution would occur if either of the joint owners were to die.

### Annuitant

The easiest way to explain the role of the *annuitant* is to compare it to the role of the insured in a life insurance contract. The annuitant is the life by which the contract is measured. Death of the annuitant may or may not trigger a payout to the beneficiary. Life contingent annuitization will be based on the annuitant's life, not the owner's. Payments may or may not go to the annuitant, depending on contract language. Otherwise the annuitant serves no other role and has no rights under the contract. In the vast majority of contracts, the owner is also the annuitant. Obviously, this greatly simplifies the arrangement.

### Beneficiary

The *beneficiary* of an annuity plays no role and has no rights under the contract until the death of *either* the annuitant or owner. As stated previously, either of those events may trigger a payout to the beneficiary. It is important to note that the beneficiary does *not* receive a stepped-up death benefit on the annuity at that time. This means that the beneficiary is responsible for all income taxes that have previously been deferred on the annuity. If the original deposit to the annuity was $10,000 and it had grown to $50,000 at the time of death, the beneficiary has the income tax burden on

## ILL. 11.6 ■ *Annuity Ownership Scenarios*

| Owner* | Annuitant* | Beneficiary | First Death | What Happens |
|---|---|---|---|---|
| SELF | SELF | SPOUSE | SELF | A, B, C, D |
| SELF | SELF | SPOUSE | SPOUSE | No impact; name new beneficiary |
| SELF | SELF | NONSPOUSE | SELF | A, B, C |
| SELF | SPOUSE | SELF | SELF | Becomes probate asset in owner's estate |

A. LUMP-SUM PAYOUT—distribution of the entire account by the end of the calendar year following the year in which death occurs. Gain taxed accordingly.

B. FIVE-YEAR RULE—requires that the beneficiary distribute the entire account by the end of the calendar year that contains the fifth anniversary of death. Gain taxed as distributions occur.

C. EXCEPTIONS TO THE FIVE-YEAR RULE—requires that the beneficiary begin payments over beneficiary's life expectancy no later than end of the calendar year following the calendar year of death. Gain taxed accordingly.

D. SPOUSAL EXCEPTION—Spouse may continue contract intact.

*There are no joint owners or joint annuitants in these examples.

$40,000. Further tax deferral of this burden is possible. For instance, the beneficiary may take a distribution over five years, over life expectancy or qualify for a spousal exception. Basically, the spousal exception allows a surviving spouse/beneficiary to take over as contractholder, continuing tax deferral. (See Ill. 11.6.) The exclusion ratio is available under any payout method.

## Completing the Application

When completing the annuity application it is very important to realize that each annuity contract is different. Some allow for joint ownership, some don't. Some allow for joint annuitants, some don't. There are different payout rules at the time of the annuitant's death. It is every practitioner's responsibility to know the contract rules for the insurer or insurers they represent and play out different scenarios with their prospects and clients, recognizing the disposition and tax consequences of each of those scenarios. The practitioner needs to know that the individual whom the contractholder/owner wants to receive the annuity proceeds in a given situation actually does receive the proceeds and has maximum tax advantages. Illustration 11.6 should help with those decisions.

## ■ 1035 EXCHANGES

Sections 1035(a)(1) and (3) of the Internal Revenue Code stipulate, in part, the following:

"No gain or loss shall be recognized on the exchange of:

- a contract of life insurance for another contract of life insurance or for an endowment or annuity contract or

- an annuity contract for an annuity contract."

The significance of this is that it allows for *tax-free exchanges* of like-kind contracts, which, in turn, provide the practitioner with a tremendous opportunity. But, like any other opportunity, it carries responsibilities. The first of these responsibilities is to know how the law works.

You may effect a tax-free exchange from one annuity to another. You may also effect a tax-free exchange from a life insurance policy to an annuity. This means that any exchange done in compliance with Section 1035 will not result in any current tax or penalties. In other words, no gain will be recognized.

For example, assume Sally purchased a deferred annuity in 1992 for $20,000 from ABC Life. It is now worth $26,000. If Sally were to become dissatisfied with ABC for solvency or renewal rate crediting reasons, she may wish to leave that contract. Assuming that she is over age 59½ and in the 31 percent tax bracket, she would net $24,140 after taxes on a full surrender, ignoring any ABC Life surrender charges. Now let's say a practitioner for XYZ Life happens to hear of Sally's plight and offers her a deferred annuity from XYZ currently paying a competitive first-year rate.

Sally becomes educated about XYZ Life and finds it to be an exceedingly strong company with impeccable financial strength and interest rate history. The practitioner for XYZ Life explains that Sally can preserve her present tax-deferred position by exchanging the ABC Life deferred annuity for the XYZ Life deferred annuity. The practitioner cautions Sally not to take possession of these funds, but instead have ABC Life surrender the annuity directly to XYZ Life. This will insure compliance with the "constructive receipt" doctrine of the Internal Revenue Code.* By following

---

\* The "constructive receipt doctrine" specifies that income that is not actually received may be taxed as if it had been, where the individual "constructively" received the income. This happens in cases where income is set aside for the individual, credited to his or her account or made available to him or her, without any substantial restrictions on his or her control over the income. The theory of this doctrine is that a person cannot "turn away" for tax purposes from income he or she has a right to receive.

this practitioner's advice, Sally nets $26,000 in this tax-free exchange transaction instead of $24,140 in a complete surrender.

Not incidentally, the XYZ Life practitioner will receive a commission. This brings us to the second responsibility in 1035 exchanges. A practitioner should move contractholders in 1035 exchanges only when it is in the best interest of the contractholder. Rolling business from one company to another (i.e., replacement) is a serious matter. Practitioners have the opportunity to earn a new commission with each exchange. Oftentimes there are surrender penalties involved. It is of paramount importance that the practitioner understand the contractholder's situation, the current product the contractholder owns and the option. The practitioner must then present the option and offer advice according to the contractholder's needs, not the practitioner's commission needs.

### Basic Rules

The following are the basic rules for 1035 exchanges:

1. The following exchanges are acceptable:

   - Life insurance to annuity

   - Flexible-premium deferred annuity to another flexible-premium deferred annuity

   - Single-premium deferred annuity to another single-premium deferred annuity

   - Flexible-premium deferred annuity to single-premium deferred annuity

   - Single-premium deferred annuity to flexible-premium deferred annuity

2. The client must not take constructive receipt of funds. Instead, the existing insurer should submit the surrendered proceeds to the new carrier.

3. Partial exchanges are not acceptable. The entire sum of the contract must go toward the new contract. No more, no less. The only exception to this is a recent tax law change that allows TSA owners to make a partial "like-kind" exchange.

■ **SUMMARY**

Quite a bit of information can be written regarding annuity taxation. What we've attempted to do in this chapter is to provide a baseline of understanding on tax law history, contract structuring and tax-free exchanges. It is extremely important that practitioners selling annuities develop an understanding of any annuity contract so that they can recognize how to structure and maintain the contract effectively to best suit a client's tax profile and parameters.

## ■ TO THE PRACTITIONER—A FINAL WORD

At the outset of this text, we commented on how complex the annuity is. As you now know, there is much more to the annuity than meets the eye. Just as asset-liability matching is vital for insurers, so too must the practitioner match annuity product design characteristics with the investment and retirement objectives of the client. Over the past few years, that task has become much easier with the advent of new product designs.

At the same time, the growth of the annuity has forced insurers to do a better job of understanding what motivates a consumer to buy and keep an annuity. Only by having a better understanding of buyer characteristics can the industry effectively provide investment support for the annuity. This will be a challenge as actuaries, asset managers and senior management of insurance companies try to differentiate between the various traditional and emerging distribution systems.

As the practitioner digests this information, putting design and marketing issues into perspective, two issues surrounding the annuity market remain of long-term concern: legislation and solvency. Throughout this text, much space and discussion were devoted to how the insurance industry protects the interests of its contractholders in order to develop a better awareness of this issue. As you have learned, the insurance industry safeguards its contractholders through a dynamic reserving system that requires insurers to maintain reserves consistent with the risks assumed in their product design and investment. It is this conservative reserving system that has earned the insurance industry the accolades of the various insurance and bond rating agencies. In fact, one major agency has called the insurance industry the most financially sound industry in our country.

As far as legislation goes, our industry will always receive politically motivated attention. This is, in part, a result of the misconception that insurers are unduly profitable and have unfair advantages over competitors. Historically, our industry lobby has been strong and united, although recently we have seen some separation of interests that has fragmented support on certain issues. Nonetheless, from change comes opportunity, and while we cannot ensure or even encourage you with regard to future legislation, we are confident that whatever changes lie ahead, the dedicated practitioner will continue to survive and thrive.

## ■ CHAPTER 11 QUESTIONS FOR REVIEW

1. The annuitant is the only party that can change the beneficiary.

   *True* or *False*

2. The "aggregation rule" does NOT apply to annuities issued after 1988.

   *True* or *False*

3. To calculate the exclusion ratio, you must know the expected return and the

   a. date of purchase.
   b. investment in the contract.
   c. tax bracket of the owner.
   d. All of the above

4. Generally speaking, the death of which of the following will trigger a full annuity distribution?

   I. Owner
   II. Owner's spouse
   III. Beneficiary
   a. I only
   b. III only
   c. I and II only
   d. II and III only

5. Which of the following is/are an exception to the 10 percent penalty for early distributions?

   a. Disability
   b. Death
   c. Substantially equal payments over life expectancy
   d. All of the above

# ····· Answer Key to Questions for Review

## CHAPTER 1

1. F
2. F
3. F
4. c
5. a

## CHAPTER 2

1. F
2. F
3. T
4. T
5. c

## CHAPTER 3

1. F
2. F
3. b
4. c
5. a
6. b

## CHAPTER 4

1. F
2. T
3. F
4. T
5. T
6. c
7. a

## CHAPTER 5

1. T
2. F
3. b
4. c
5. d
6. b

## CHAPTER 6

1. T
2. F
3. F
4. T
5. c
6. d

## CHAPTER 7

1. F
2. F
3. c
4. c

## CHAPTER 8

1. d
2. F
3. d
4. a
5. d

## CHAPTER 9

1. T
2. F
3. T
4. b
5. d

## CHAPTER 10

1. F
2. F
3. d
4. a
5. d

## CHAPTER 11

1. F
2. F
3. b
4. b
5. d

# ...... Appendix

T his appendix contains a sample flexible premium deferred annuity contract. It is representative of a typical contract issued by annuity carriers and reflects standard language and provisions found in actual contracts.

# SUPERIOR MUTUAL LIFE INSURANCE COMPANY OF AMERICA

Flexible Premium
Deferred Annuity Policy

Premiums Acceptable During the
Lifetime of the Annuitant and prior
to the Annuity Date

Guaranteed Annuity Values

Options for Payment of Proceeds

Not Eligible for Dividends

This Policy is issued in consideration of the statement contained in the application and the payment of the Premium.

*Jacob Carson*
_____
President

*Richard Plitt*
_____
Secretary

**10-DAY RIGHT TO EXAMINE POLICY**
Within 10 days after this policy is first received, the Owner may cancel it for any reason by delivering or mailing it to the agent through whom it was purchased, or the Home Office of the Company. Upon cancellation, the Company will return any premium paid.

**Policy Provisions**

**Alphabetical Guide**

# Superior Mutual Life Insurance Company

| | |
|---|---|
| Policy Number: | 000-00-0000 |
| Annuitant: | John Williams |
| Issue Age: | 35 |
| Issue Date: | October 1, 1992 |
| Annuity Date: | October 1, 2022 |
| Owner: | The Annuitant |
| Initial Premium: | $10,000 |
| Planned Periodic Premiums: | $1,000 annually |
| Beneficiary: | As Designated in the Application Unless Subsequently Changed |

## TABLE OF GUARANTEED PAID-UP ANNUITY COMMENCING
## AT POLICY ANNIVERSARY FOLLOWING 65TH BIRTHDAY

(Assuming Level Annual Premiums of $1,000 each, received at the beginning of each policy year.)

| Age at Issue | Monthly Income for 120 Months Certain and Life Thereafter | |
| --- | --- | --- |
| | Males | Females |
| 25 | $629.53 | $569.24 |
| 26 | 598.94 | 541.59 |
| 27 | 569.54 | 515.00 |
| 28 | 541.26 | 489.43 |
| 29 | 514.07 | 464.85 |
| 30 | 487.93 | 441.21 |
| 31 | 462.79 | 418.48 |
| 32 | 438.62 | 396.62 |
| 33 | 415.38 | 375.61 |
| 34 | 393.04 | 355.40 |
| 35 | 371.55 | 335.97 |
| 36 | 350.89 | 317.29 |
| 37 | 331.03 | 299.33 |
| 38 | 311.92 | 282.05 |
| 39 | 293.56 | 265.45 |
| 40 | 275.90 | 249.48 |
| 41 | 258.91 | 234.12 |
| 42 | 242.59 | 219.36 |
| 43 | 225.89 | 205.16 |
| 44 | 211.79 | 191.51 |
| 45 | 197.27 | 178.38 |
| 46 | 183.32 | 165.76 |
| 47 | 169.90 | 153.63 |
| 48 | 156.99 | 141.96 |
| 49 | 144.58 | 130.74 |
| 50 | 132.65 | 119.95 |
| 51 | 121.18 | 109.58 |
| 52 | 110.15 | 99.60 |
| 53 | 99.54 | 90.01 |
| 54 | 89.34 | 80.79 |
| 55 | 79.54 | 71.92 |
| 56 | 70.11 | 63.40 |
| 57 | 61.04 | 55.20 |
| 58 | 52.32 | 47.31 |
| 59 | 43.94 | 39.73 |
| 60 | 35.88 | 32.45 |
| 61 | 28.13 | 25.44 |
| 62 | 20.68 | 18.70 |
| 63 | 13.51 | 12.22 |
| 64 | 6.62 | 5.99 |

*Example:* If you started paying $2,000 per policy year commencing at age 35 and stopped paying premium at age 50 after 15 years of such payments, you could compute your paid-up annuity payments as follows:

| | | | | |
| --- | --- | --- | --- | --- |
| Age 35: Male – | $ 371.55 | | Female – | $ 335.97 |
| Age 50: Male – | (–) 132.65 | | Female – | (–) 119.95 |
| | $ 238.90 | | | $ 216.02 |
| Level Annual Premium | × 2 | | | × 2 |
| 1,000 | = $ 477.80 | | | = $ 432.04 |

This does not include additional income which may result from the excess interest credited or improved annuity rates available when you reach age 65.

Page 4

## PREMIUM PROVISIONS

### Premium Payments

The initial premium is shown in the Schedule. If no further premiums are paid in subsequent policy years, the company may charge an administrative fee of the lesser of $25 or the excess interest credited during the policy year. The charge is made at the end of each such policy year. The fee will be waived, however, if the then Accumulated Value exceeds $2,500.

### Planned Periodic Premiums

Additional premium payments may be made at any time. Failure to pay such additional premium will not alter or waive any terms of the contract. No further premium payments are required to provide annuity benefits on the Annuity Date. Notices may be sent Annually, Semi-Annually or Quarterly. The Owner may request the Company to send premium notices. Premium Payments may also be made by automatic monthly transfers from an established checking account. A change in frequency may be made at any time.

The Company reserves the right to refuse initial payments of less than $1,000, or subsequent payments of less than $50.00 each. It may also refuse to accept payments more frequently than monthly. Payments in excess of $100,000 in any policy year may be made only with the Company's prior written approval.

## GENERAL PROVISIONS

CONTRACT. This policy (and application) is the entire contract between you and us. A copy of the application is attached. It is a part of this policy. Statements in the application are deemed representations and not warranties. No such statement shall void or be used in defense of a claim unless in the written application. No person except the President, Vice President, Secretary or Assistant Secretary has the power to change, modify or waive the provisions of this contract. Such changes must be made in writing.

This policy is issued in consideration of the completed application and payment of the premium as determined by the Company.

NON-PARTICIPATING. This Policy does not participate in the profits or surplus of the Company.

ANNUITANT. The Annuitant is the person named as Annuitant on Page 3.

JOINT ANNUITANT. The Joint Annuitant is the person named in the application as the Joint Annuitant.

JOINT OWNERS. Husband and wife may own this policy jointly. Joint owners are as named in the application and on page 3.

OWNERSHIP AND CONTROL. The Owner of this Policy is the Annuitant unless otherwise stated in the application or as changed later by request. All rights of ownership of this Policy terminate at the death of the Annuitant. Consistent with the Beneficiary's rights and any assignment, the Owner may, during the lifetime of the Annuitant:

1. assign or surrender this Policy;

2. amend this Policy with the consent of the Company; and

3. exercise any right conferred by this Policy.

INCONTESTABILITY. This policy shall be incontestable from the issue date.

ASSIGNMENTS. The Company shall have notice of an assignment when the original assignment or a duplicate is filed in the Company's Home Office. The Company will not assume any responsibility for the validity of an assignment. Before payment of the policy, the claim of an assignee shall be subject to our satisfaction.

### Death Benefit Before Annuity Date

The Company will pay a benefit upon receipt of due proof of the death of either the annuitant or the owner. The proceeds are the amount of premiums paid less withdrawals, or the Accumulated Value of the Policy, if greater.

If any Owner dies, and the Owner's spouse is neither the Beneficiary nor a surviving joint owner, the proceeds of this policy will be payable as:

1. a lump sum;

2. over a period not to exceed 60 months from the date of death; or

3. as a life annuity based on the Beneficiary's life expectancy. The proceeds must be used within one year of the death to provide for the annuity.

The proceeds payable upon the death of the Owner shall be paid to the Beneficiary, if living; otherwise, to the Owner's estate.

If an Owner dies before the Annuity Date, and the Owner's spouse is the Beneficiary or a surviving joint Owner, the policy will continue.

If the Annuitant who is not an Owner dies, the proceeds will be paid in one sum to the Beneficiary or be applied under any one of the Payment Options.

### Beneficiary

The Beneficiary is named in the application. The Beneficiary may be changed by written request. The request must be on a form satisfactory to the Company. It must be signed by the Owner. It will relate back and take effect as of the date of the written request subject to any payment made by the Company before the request was recorded. The Company shall be relieved of liability to the extent of any payment made by it before such record.

### Death Benefit After Annuity Date

If either the Annuitant or the Owner dies after the Annuity Date the annuity payment will continue as provided for under the Annuity Option then in effect.

### Age

Age in this Policy means age last birthday.

### Contract Years

Contract Years and Anniversaries will be measured from the Issue Date.

### Evidence That Annuitant Is Living

The Company shall have the right to require proof the Annuitant is living on the date of any annuity payment.

### Misstatement of Age or Sex

If the age or sex of the Annuitant has been misstated, the benefits under this Policy will be those which the premiums paid would have purchased for the correct age and sex. Any payment adjustment will be made against succeeding payments. It will include interest charged or credited at not less than 4 percent per annum.

## ACCUMULATED VALUES

### Crediting Premium Payments

All premium payments, less premium tax, and less administrative fees, if any, shall be credited to the Accumulated Value. This credit shall be called the Net Premium. Tax on Annuity premiums is determined initially by the state in which the policy is delivered. If no premium tax is deducted but later determined due any state, it will be deducted from the Accumulated Value.

### Excess Interest

The Accumulated Value may be credited with interest in excess of the guaranteed rate of 4 percent. On any policy anniversary the excess interest rate will be set on the Accumulated Value as of that policy anniversary and guaranteed until the next policy anniversary. Premiums received during a policy year will be credited with interest at the rate then in effect on newly issued policies until the next policy anniversary.

### Interest Credits

Interest will be credited from the day Premium Payments are received by the Company at its Home Office.

### Accumulated Value

The Accumulated Value is the sum of:

1. the Net Premiums, as described in the section "Crediting Premium Payments";

2. increased by the total of interest credits at the guaranteed rate of 4 percent per annum and any excess interest which may be credited to that account; and

3. reduced by any amounts withdrawn.

## RIGHTS OF WITHDRAWAL AND SURRENDER

The Owner has the right to withdraw Accumulated Values from this policy at any time subject to the charge for early surrender described on page 7 upon written request to the Company. The Company may, however, insist upon complete surrender if such withdrawal would reduce the Accumulated Value below one thousand dollars ($1,000).

The Policy may be surrendered for the entire Cash Surrender Value by presenting the Policy to the Company at its Home Office. Cash Surrender Value is equal to Accumulated Value less any applicable surrender charge.

Any Surrender or Withdrawal is subject to the charge for Early Surrender rules stated below.

Surrender charge, if any is then applicable, would be waived on the Annuity Date. Surrender charge will also be waived if the Accumulated Value is used to purchase a life annuity with the Company.

The Company may defer payment of the Cash Surrender Value for a period of not more than six months.

### Partial Withdrawals Without Charge

Up to 20 percent of the then total accumulated value may be withdrawn at any time without Charge For Early Surrender during the first contract year. This percentage will reduce to 10 percent for renewal years. One partial withdrawal may be made in each policy year.

### Charge for Early Surrender and Partial Withdrawal in Excess of Partial Withdrawal Limit

Except as provided in "Partial Withdrawals Without Charge," if Accumulated Values are withdrawn, or the policy is surrendered prior to the Annuity Date, the following charge shall be made against the amount of the Accumulated Value withdrawn or surrendered. The charge is expressed as a percentage of the amount withdrawn. It is based upon the policy year in which the withdrawal or surrender occurs. (See Tables D and E, pages 9 and 10.)

| Policy Year | Surrender Charges as a Percent of Accumulated Value Withdrawn in Excess of Penalty-Free Partial Withdrawal Limit |
|---|---|
| 1 | 10% |
| 2 | 9 |
| 3 | 8 |
| 4 | 7 |
| 5 | 6 |
| 6 | 5 |
| 7 | 4 |
| 8 | 3 |
| 9 | 2 |
| 10 | 1 |
| Thereafter | 0 |

### Minimum Benefits

The paid-up annuity value, cash surrender value and the amount payable at death under this Policy are not less than the minimum benefits required by law of the state in which this Policy is delivered.

## PAYMENT OPTIONS—FORM OF ANNUITY

### Payment Options

On the Annuity Date, the Owner may select any of the Payment Options shown below. If no Option is selected, payment will be made as provided in the section "Automatic Option." Prior to the Annuity Date, the Owner may apply the Accumulated Value, less surrender charges, if any, under these payment options. The date payments begin will be the Option Date.

### Payment Certificate

At the time Proceeds become payable under a Payment Option, a Payment Certificate will be issued to the payee in exchange for the Policy. Its effective date will be the Option Date.

Payment Certificates may not be assigned.

### Guaranteed and Excess Interest

Payment Options listed below are based on 4 percent interest compounded annually age last birthday. The tables following illustrate payments at that interest rate. The Company may offer annuity benefits based upon rates more favorable than those illustrated. It will generally be to the advantage of the person selecting the Payment Option to inquire as to the current rate.

### Death of Payee

If any payments remain to be paid under a Payment Option at the death of the Payee, payment will be made under the terms of the Payment Certificate.

### Amount of Annuity

The guaranteed amount of annuity payable will be no less than that shown in the Annuity Tables following.

Monthly amounts of life income are shown for each $1,000 of guaranteed value applied. If the payments are less than $20 each, we may require you choose a different payment interval.

Payment Options may be credited with Excess Interest. The actual amount of annuity payable may therefore be more. Also, payment options with higher guaranteed minimums than those shown may be in use by the Company at the time proceeds are payable. If so, the more favorable Payment Options will be available.

OPTION 1. Payment of a Designated Amount: The Company will make equal monthly, quarterly, semiannual or annual payments. The payment elected must be at least $60 a year for each $1,000 of Proceeds applied. Payments will continue until the Proceeds applied and interest at 4 percent and any additional interest are exhausted.

OPTION 2. Payment for a Designated Number of Years: Payments will continue for the number of years elected, not to exceed 30. Payments may be increased by additional interest. (See Table A.)

OPTION 3. Payment of Life Income: Payments will continue for the lifetime of the Annuitant or, if Proceeds Upon Death are applied under this Option, of the Beneficiary. The amount of payment will depend upon the age and sex of the payee at the time the first payment is due. Payment will be subject to proof of age. The Company reserves the right to require proof that the payee is alive at the time each payment is due. Payments are guaranteed (certain) for 10 or 20 years, as elected, and for life thereafter.

In the event of the death of the payee during the guaranteed period, payments will continue for the balance of the Period in accordance with the payment certificate. Additional interest may be paid or credited during the guaranteed period of 10 or 20 years as determined by the Company. (See Table B.)

OPTION 4. Joint or Survivor Life Income. Payment will be made to the Annuitants while both the Annuitant and Joint Annuitant are living. Payments will continue to the survivor during the remaining lifetime of the survivor. (See Table C.)

OTHER. Other methods of settlement may be arranged by agreement with the Company.

AUTOMATIC OPTION: If no Option has been selected by the Annuity Date, the then current Accumulated Value will be applied under Option 3: Life Income with 10 years guaranteed.

### TABLE A
### LIMITED INSTALLMENTS

**AMOUNT OF INSTALLMENT PER $1,000 OF PROCEEDS**

| Number Years Payable | Annual | Semi-Annual | Quarterly | Monthly | Number Years Payable | Annual | Semi-Annual | Quarterly | Monthly |
|---|---|---|---|---|---|---|---|---|---|
| 1 | $1,000.00 | $504.90 | $253.69 | $84.84 | 11 | $109.76 | $55.42 | $27.84 | $9.31 |
| 2 | 509.80 | 257.40 | 129.33 | 43.25 | 12 | 102.45 | 51.73 | 25.99 | 8.69 |
| 3 | 346.49 | 174.94 | 87.90 | 29.40 | 13 | 96.29 | 48.62 | 24.43 | 8.17 |
| 4 | 264.89 | 133.75 | 67.20 | 22.47 | 14 | 91.03 | 45.96 | 23.09 | 7.72 |
| 5 | 215.99 | 109.05 | 54.79 | 18.32 | 15 | 86.48 | 43.66 | 21.94 | 7.34 |
| 6 | 183.42 | 92.61 | 46.53 | 15.56 | 16 | 82.52 | 41.66 | 20.93 | 7.00 |
| 7 | 160.20 | 80.89 | 40.64 | 13.59 | 17 | 79.64 | 39.91 | 20.05 | 6.71 |
| 8 | 142.82 | 72.11 | 36.23 | 12.17 | 18 | 75.96 | 38.35 | 19.27 | 6.44 |
| 9 | 129.32 | 66.29 | 32.81 | 10.97 | 19 | 73.21 | 36.96 | 18.57 | 6.21 |
| 10 | 118.55 | 59.86 | 30.07 | 10.06 | 20 | 20.75 | 35.72 | 17.95 | 6.00 |

### TABLE B
### CONTINUOUS INSTALLMENTS

Amount of Installments Payable for Life per $1,000 of Proceeds.

| Age of Male Payee* | 120 Months Certain | 240 Months Certain | Age of Female Payee* | 120 Months Certain | 240 Months Certain |
|---|---|---|---|---|---|
| 55 | $5.16 | $4.86 | 55 | $4.74 | $4.59 |
| 56 | 5.26 | 4.92 | 56 | 4.82 | 4.65 |
| 57 | 5.36 | 4.98 | 57 | 4.90 | 4.71 |
| 58 | 5.47 | 5.04 | 58 | 4.99 | 4.77 |
| 59 | 5.58 | 5.10 | 59 | 5.08 | 4.84 |
| 60 | 5.69 | 5.16 | 60 | 5.18 | 4.90 |
| 61 | 5.82 | 5.22 | 61 | 5.29 | 4.97 |
| 62 | 5.95 | 5.27 | 62 | 5.40 | 5.03 |
| 63 | 6.08 | 5.33 | 63 | 5.51 | 5.10 |
| 64 | 6.22 | 5.38 | 64 | 5.63 | 5.17 |
| 65 | 6.37 | 5.43 | 65 | 5.76 | 5.23 |
| 66 | 6.52 | 5.48 | 66 | 5.90 | 5.29 |
| 67 | 6.68 | 5.52 | 67 | 6.04 | 5.35 |
| 68 | 6.84 | 5.56 | 68 | 6.19 | 5.41 |
| 69 | 7.00 | 5.60 | 69 | 6.35 | 5.46 |
| 70 | 7.17 | 5.63 | 70 | 6.51 | 5.51 |

*Annuity Rates for ages not shown in Table B are available on request from the Company.
  Basis for values in Table B is the 1983 "a" Mortality Table at 4 percent interest, age last birthday.

## TABLE C
## JOINT AND 100 PERCENT SURVIVOR ANNUITY

Amount of Installments Payable for Joint and 100 Percent Survivor for Life per $1,000 of Proceeds.

| Male Age | Female Age | | | | |
|---|---|---|---|---|---|
| | 55 | 60 | 62 | 65 | 70 |
| 55 | $4.34 | $4.52 | $4.59 | $4.69 | $4.84 |
| 60 | 4.45 | 4.69 | 4.79 | 4.93 | 5.16 |
| 62 | 4.49 | 4.75 | 4.86 | 5.03 | 5.30 |
| 65 | 4.54 | 4.83 | 4.96 | 5.17 | 5.51 |
| 70 | 4.60 | 4.95 | 5.11 | 5.37 | 5.84 |

Basis for values is the 1983 "a" Mortality Table at 4 percent interest, age last birthday.

Values not shown in Table C will be furnished upon request.

### GUARANTEED VALUES

The tables below illustrate the guaranteed values for a single deposit $1,000 (Table D) and a series of annual deposits of $1,000 each (Table E). An extension of this table beyond the years shown is available from the Company upon request.

The Company will report the actual amount of Accumulated Value to the Owner annually. Notice will be mailed to the last known address of the Owner.

## TABLE D
## GUARANTEED VALUES OF A SINGLE $1,000 PREMIUM PAID ON THE ISSUE DATE

Guaranteed Interest Rate 4 Percent

| End of Policy Year | Accumulated Value | Surrender Charge | | | Cash Surrender Value |
|---|---|---|---|---|---|
| | | Percent | Proportion of Accumulated Value Subject to Charge | Charge | |
| 1 | $1,040.00 | 10% | 80% | $83.20 | $ 956.80 |
| 2 | 1,081.60 | 9 | 90 | 87.61 | 993.99 |
| 3 | 1,124.86 | 8 | 90 | 80.99 | 1,043.87 |
| 4 | 1,169.86 | 7 | 90 | 73.70 | 1,096.16 |
| 5 | 1,216.65 | 6 | 90 | 65.70 | 1,150.95 |
| 6 | 1,265.32 | 5 | 90 | 56.94 | 1,208.38 |
| 7 | 1,315.93 | 4 | 90 | 47.37 | 1,268.56 |
| 8 | 1,368.57 | 3 | 90 | 36.95 | 1,331.62 |
| 9 | 1,423.31 | 2 | 90 | 25.62 | 1,397.69 |
| 10 | 1,480.24 | 1 | 90 | 13.32 | 1,466.92 |
| 11 | 1,539.45 | 0 | 0 | 0 | 1,539.45 |
| 12 | 1,601.03 | 0 | 0 | 0 | 1,601.03 |
| 13 | 1,665.07 | 0 | 0 | 0 | 1,665.07 |
| 14 | 1,731.68 | 0 | 0 | 0 | 1,731.68 |
| 15 | 1,800.94 | 0 | 0 | 0 | 1,800.94 |
| 16 | 1,872.98 | 0 | 0 | 0 | 1,872.98 |
| 17 | 1,947.90 | 0 | 0 | 0 | 1,947.90 |
| 18 | 2,025.82 | 0 | 0 | 0 | 2,025.82 |
| 19 | 2,106.85 | 0 | 0 | 0 | 2,106.85 |
| 20 | 2,191.12 | 0 | 0 | 0 | 2,191.12 |

## TABLE E
## GUARANTEED VALUES OF A SINGLE $1,000 PREMIUMS
## PAID AT THE START OF EACH POLICY YEAR

Guaranteed Interest Rate 4 Percent

| End of Policy Year | Accumulated Value | Surrender Charge | | | Cash Surrender Value |
|---|---|---|---|---|---|
| | | Percent | Proportion of Accumulated Value Subject to Charge | Charge | |
| 1 | $ 1,040.00 | 10% | 80% | $ 83.20 | $ 956.80 |
| 2 | 2,121.60 | 9 | 90 | 171.85 | 1,949.75 |
| 3 | 3,246.46 | 8 | 90 | 233.74 | 3,012.72 |
| 4 | 4,416.32 | 7 | 90 | 278.23 | 4,138.09 |
| 5 | 5,632.98 | 6 | 90 | 304.19 | 5,328.79 |
| 6 | 6,898.29 | 5 | 90 | 310.42 | 6,587.87 |
| 7 | 8,214.23 | 4 | 90 | 295.72 | 7,918.51 |
| 8 | 9,582.80 | 3 | 90 | 258.74 | 9,324.06 |
| 9 | 11,006.11 | 2 | 90 | 198.11 | 10,808.00 |
| 10 | 12,486.35 | 1 | 90 | 112.38 | 12,373.97 |
| 11 | 14,025.81 | 0 | 0 | 0 | 14,025.81 |
| 12 | 15,626.84 | 0 | 0 | 0 | 15,626.84 |
| 13 | 17,291.91 | 0 | 0 | 0 | 17,291.91 |
| 14 | 19,023.59 | 0 | 0 | 0 | 19,023.59 |
| 15 | 20,824.53 | 0 | 0 | 0 | 20,824.53 |
| 16 | 22,697.51 | 0 | 0 | 0 | 22,697.51 |
| 17 | 24,645.41 | 0 | 0 | 0 | 24,645.41 |
| 18 | 26,671.23 | 0 | 0 | 0 | 26,671.23 |
| 19 | 28,778.08 | 0 | 0 | 0 | 28,778.08 |
| 20 | 30,969.20 | 0 | 0 | 0 | 30,969.20 |